SOMERSET RAILWAYS

SOMERSET RAILWAYS

Colin G Maggs

Somerset Books

Acknowledgement

I would like to thank Colin Roberts and Robert Dunning sincerely for checking and improving the text.

First published in Great Britain in 2007

British Library Cataloguing-in-Publication Data.
A CIP record for this title is available from the British Library.

ISBN 978 0 86183 442 6

SOMERSET BOOKS
Somerset Books is a partnership between DAA Halsgrove
and Somerset County Council (Directorate of Culture and Heritage)
www.somerset.gov.uk

Halsgrove House
Ryelands Industrial Estate,
Bagley Road, Wellington
Somerset TA21 9PZ
Tel: 01823 653777
Fax: 01823 216796
E-mail: sales@halsgrove.com
Website: www.halsgrove.com

Printed and bound in Great Britain by
CPI Antony Rowe Ltd., Chippenham, Wiltshire

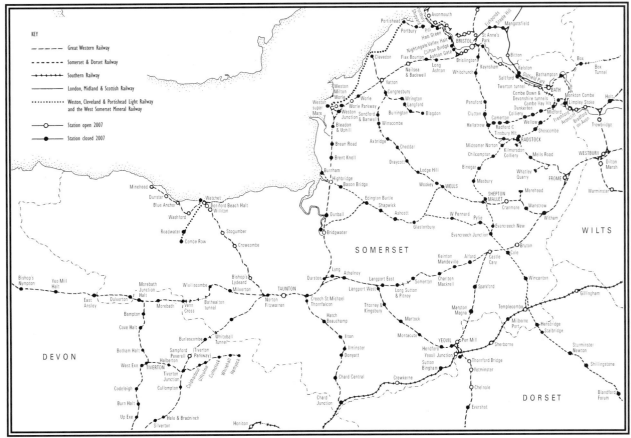

A detailed map of the Weston, Clevedon & Portishead Railway may be found on page 147

Contents

1 Early Railways

MANY PEOPLE feel a thrill as an express passes, even if today it happens to be a HST rather than a train of tea- and cream-coloured coaches drawn by a gleaming 'Castle', or a line of malachite-green coaches drawn by a sparkling 'Merchant Navy'. Even the humble branch-line train had a charm and character of its own. But what is the story behind those lines, active or derelict? How did they come into being and develop?

The first railway in Somerset, indeed one of the first in the world, was very much a local line. Early in the 18th century Ralph Allen bought the right to quarry stone on Combe Down, near Bath. Possessing a good business sense, he realised that in order to make a reasonable profit, a way had to be devised to transport large blocks of stone weighing upwards of four tons from the quarries to a wharf he had built on the River Avon at Widcombe, 1½ miles away and 500 feet below. There the stone could be sold to builders who were rapidly expanding

Wagons descending Ralph Allen's railway from Combe Down to the River Avon at Bath, *c* 1737. His mansion, Prior Park, is in the centre. (Author's collection)

Bath, or shipped to Bristol down the Avon which had recently been made navigable, and then taken onwards to Dublin and Belfast, thereby breaking the monopoly of Portland stone. The state of the roads and the gradients made transport by traditional sledge or cart almost impracticable, and Allen's solution was a railway. It was not an entirely novel idea as he had seen railways in Northumberland while on his travels in connection with the postal service.

Opened in 1731, from Combe Down Allen's railway descended on an incline of 1 in 10 down a new road, now known as Ralph Allen's Drive. The timber rails, probably of oak, were set at a gauge of 3ft 9in. The wagons, each costing over £30, were also of oak and had low detachable sides and short, upright ends. The precursors of the modern low-sided goods wagons, they ran on four cast-iron spoked wheels with deep flanges, the latter an innovation as hitherto the rails, not the wheels, had been flanged. Two horses drew the trucks on level ground or an empty wagon up hill, but loaded vehicles descended by gravity and an efficient braking system was provided. Each front wheel could be locked by bolts passing through the spokes and those brakes were manipulated by iron rods leading to handles at the rear. Either hind wheel could be locked by a 'Jigg Pole' pressed down by a chain that could be tightened from the back and held by a rachet and pawl. The railway enabled stone to be delivered at the wharf for 7s 6d a ton, a worthwhile reduction from the 10s previously charged.

When the building of houses in the North and South Parades in Bath was begun in 1739, rails were laid on the north side of the Avon and loaded trucks were carried over on barges and hauled up by capstan: Ralph Allen had invented the first train ferry.

The wharf beside the Avon can be seen lower left; crane is lowering a stone block into a barge, 1734. (Author's collection)

A wagon used on Ralph Allen's railway. Notice the brake gear. (Author's collection)

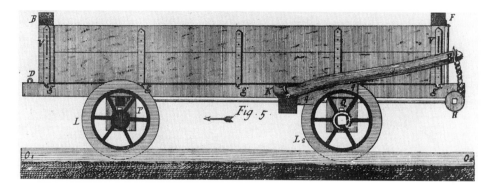

In 1755 Allen laid the foundation stone of the Palladian Bridge below his home, Prior Park. It was sited in a combe, well below the level of his railway. To reach the bridge works a self-acting incline was built, a descending loaded wagon drawing up an empty. He had scored another 'first'.

Allen died on 29 June 1764 and shortly afterwards his railway was dismantled. The idea was not forgotten and some thirty years later, when the Kennet & Avon Canal was cut, double-acting inclines were built linking quarries with the canal. One of those inclines was the second railway in Somerset. The *Bath Chronicle* of 23 June 1808 carried an advertisement for 'Any Person or Persons willing to contract to make an inclined Plane Road from Bathampton Quarries to the Kennet and Avon Canal ... are desired to send their proposals (sealed up) to Mr Bennet, engineer, St James Parade, Bath'.

That 'inclined plane road' was a sloping railway 2658 ft in length, on which the weight of the descending loaded wagons drew up the empties, both trains of wagons being connected by a rope passing around a wheel at the summit that allowed the speed to be regulated. P. Egan in his book *Walking through Bath*, published in 1816, describes the line: there is 'an iron railway, from the immense steep height ... It is curious to observe the iron carriages sent up and down without horses; and by aid of machinery the vehicles change their positions midway, the full one running down to the barge at the canal, and the empty one making its way to the top again to receive its load'. The line opened in 1810 and the *Bath Guide* of 1810—11 noted 'the immense quantities of stone conveyed by the inclined plane from the quarries of Messrs Bowsher & Co to the canal'. The line was derelict by 1847.

Although closed 160 years ago, traces can be seen today. From the wharf below the A36 Warminster road where the Kennet & Avon Canal was made wider to allow a barge to lay by, it is still possible to see the railway's formation leading up on a shelf cut in the hillside to the site of the Dry Arch. It received that name because, at the time of building, most bridges were across water and those across land were rare indeed. The arch was demolished in 1958 to allow a road improvement easing a dangerous corner.

South of the A36 the railway to Hampton Down, now a public footpath, crosses a small bridge partly repaired in red brick and from here onwards to the summit many stone sleeper blocks can still be seen. Plate rails were used, a reverse concept to that used by Network Rail today. Instead of a flanged wheel running on a smooth rail, on a plateway an ordinary plain wheel ran on a flanged rail. The cast iron plate rails measured 2½ ft in length and were fixed to stone sleeper blocks by spikes and wooden plugs. The gauge was 3ft 4in.

Two Prussian mining engineers, von Oeynhausen and von Dechen, visiting the railway in 1826 or 1827 wrote: 'These rails are too weak for the load which is lowered upon them, which amounts to 80cwt including the wagon. This is proved by the large heaps of broken rails that lie beside the line; nevertheless, the newly-delivered rails are cast no stronger'. The three later types of rail were significantly more substantial.

The Prussians described the rolling stock: 'The wagons on which up to 70 cwt of stone is loaded consist of a wooden platform provided with an iron railing 2½ ft high. The platform is composed of four frame-beams 7½ ft long, 7in high and 5in thick, bound together by four cross-beams and some iron cramps ... One such wagon with its wheels weighs 10cwt. The narrow wheels probably contribute greatly to the number of broken rails'.

The railway was worked in two sections: one was 330yd in length from the canal wharf to just south of the Dry Arch and had a uniform inclination of about 5 degrees; the other was 550yd long and varied from a gentle slope near the top to about 10 degrees in the middle and at the bottom was both inclined and curved.

The first locomotive-worked railway in Somerset linked Radstock with the Somerset Coal Canal at Midford. The story of the line really started in 1792 when the owners of collieries south of Bath wanted to expand their market. Road transport was unsatisfactory for the cost of carrying coal to Bath or Bristol was rather more than the actual pithead price, thus doubling the cost of fuel to those living away from the collieries.

Arch carrying the inclined plane linking quarries on Hampton Down with the Kennet & Avon Canal. This arch is across a path immediately south of the Dry Arch, 16 February 1977. (Author)

The Dry Arch which carried the inclined plane. This photograph was taken on 16 April 1954 shortly before the arch was removed when the A36 was widened. It was known as the 'Dry Arch' because at the time of its construction most bridges were across waterways. (Author)

Remains of the stone wharf on the Kennet & Avon Canal near Holcombe Farm, Bathampton. It was served by the railway from Hampton Down. On 16 February 1977 a horse is standing on the former inclined plane. (Author)

A canal was the answer to the problem because one horse could draw 25 tons in a canal boat but only a ton or so on roads when it had to tackle the hills between the pits and Bath. Thus the Somerset Coal Canal was planned. It was agreed that it required two arms. From a junction with the Kennet & Avon Canal at Dundas Aqueduct it would run to Midford, where one arm would proceed to the valley below Timsbury while the other led to a terminal basin at Radstock immediately south of the present Waldegrave Arms Hotel.

Contracts were let in 1795 and the work of cutting the 7-mile canal began. The principal features of the Radstock arm were a 405yd tunnel beneath the Wellow Brook to the Hinton Charterhouse road near Wellow church, and an aqueduct over the Cam Brook at Midford.

The national financial crisis in 1799 cast a shadow over the project. Most of the cash that Parliament had authorised to be raised had been spent, yet the canal was far from complete. The Radstock branch was at a higher level than the Timsbury arm and it was intended linking them at Midford by a series of locks that would have been very expensive. This was obviated by bringing in an economy measure – a mile-long railway from Twinhoe to Midford to connect the two levels.

The Radstock branch of the Somerset Coal Canal was opened in 1804 but was very little used, probably because of the inconvenience and expense of the quadruple transhipment of coal from railway to canal at Radstock, from canal to railway at Twinhoe, from railway to canal at Midford and finally from canal to road at Bath. A 25-ton coal barge owned by John Maggs worked the length between Radstock and Twinhoe, but ceased when his bankruptcy forced him to sell the vessel in 1811 when it was described as 'nearly new' – the phrase suggesting that it had seen little use.

The omission of mention of the Radstock arm from an advertisement seeking tenders for the maintenance of the Somerset Coal Canal in 1812 leads one to conjecture that this section was probably disused at that date. Another reason claimed for its demise was that the owners of the riparian rights on the Somer stream objected to their water being diverted to feed the canal, and since other sources were insufficient to fill it abandonment was the only course.

The need for good transport between the coalfield and Bath still needed fulfilling. At a meeting on 1 October 1814 it was decided that a railway would be built along the towpath of the canal between Radstock and Midford. Only two transhipments would be required: from railway to canal at Midford and from canal to road at Bath. Like the Hampton Down line, it was the plates that were flanged, the trucks having plain wheels capable of running on ordinary roads or the rail road with equal facility.

The work of laying the track proceeded very quickly and on 20 July 1815 the *Bath Chronicle* announced: '… the completion of the New Rail Road, from the village of Radstoke (*sic*) to the canal near Midford, a distance of upwards of seven miles; by which means a certain and regular communication is now

The south portal of the Somerset Coal Canal railway tunnel at Wellow, 11 August 1998. The tunnel mouth is now in a private garden. (Author)

'The Gug' at Clandown: a branch tramroad that fed the Somerset Coal Canal Railway. (*Bath & County Graphic*, May 1898)

William Ashman, engineer, Clandown Colliery. (Author's collection)

opened to the several great collieries of Radstoke, Welton, Clandown and Smallcombe, from which works a constant supply of the very best Somersetshire coal may now be depended on to any extent'.

Three horses drew eight or nine wagons holding 27 cwt each. The whole journey from Radstock to Midford and back took five hours, which meant that two double trips could be made each day. At the height of the railway's fortunes no less than 28 return trips were required daily. The ruins of the stables where the railway horses were kept may still be seen west of Midford Viaduct, just by the aqueduct where a short arm from the main canal crosses the Cam Brook to the transhipment wharves.

The Radstock Railway was a single line, and passing loops were provided at 600yd intervals. When the inevitable happened and trains met head-on away from a crossing loop, the drivers took their coats off and fought it out, the winner taking precedence. On Saturdays the wagons known as 'tubs' were brushed out, boards were placed across them and the vehicles conveyed people from Midford, Wellow and Single Hill to and from Radstock market. That was certainly one of the very first passenger railways in the country.

In August 1826 and three years before Stephenson's *Rocket* appeared on the Liverpool & Manchester Railway, William Ashman, the engineer of Clandown Colliery, built a steam locomotive which was able to draw nine loaded wagons between Clandown and Midford. It reached a speed of 3¾ mph on the level but unfortunately proved a failure simply because its weight of 2 tons 3 cwt broke the cast iron plates. Mechanically it was sound and ended its life as a stationary steam engine at Clandown.

Later in the 19th century much of the coal traffic from the area was siphoned off by the Great Western Railway's branch from Radstock to Frome and by the Bristol & North Somerset Railway's line from Bristol. Then in the 1870s the canal proprietors were pleased to hear that the Somerset & Dorset Railway proposed building a line across the Mendips from Evercreech to Bath and managed to sell their almost redundant railway for £20,000 to be used as a trackbed. Because of its ancestry that section of the Somerset & Dorset from Midford to Radstock was very sinuous and flange oilers were provided to ease rolling stock round the sharp curves.

William Ashman's tombstone in Clandown churchyard. (Author)

2 An Outline Survey of Railways in Somerset

THE RAILWAY map of Somerset looks complicated, but is easier to comprehend when the history of the lines is understood. The first main line in the county opened between Bath and Bristol with Isambard Kingdom Brunel as its engineer. Brunel favoured the broad gauge of 7ft 0¼in between the rails, offering a stable and safe ride and larger and therefore more economic wagons with space for powerful locomotives.

Although the Great Western Railway originally terminated at Bristol, an associated company, the Bristol & Exeter Railway, also with Brunel as its engineer, extended the line westwards. Another broad gauge company, the Wilts, Somerset & Weymouth Railway, ran from Thingley Junction near Chippenham to Weymouth, the line running through Somerset for approximately half its length. Several local companies were set up to build branches to those broad gauge lines.

South Somerset was served by the London & South Western Railway, a standard gauge line with 4ft 8½in between the rails. In the north of the county another standard gauge line, the Midland Railway, ran to Bath. It seems obvious that the two standard gauge lines should be linked and that was done by the Somerset & Dorset Railway.

Although the choice of gauge mattered little in the early days of

GWR broad gauge and standard gauge locomotives: left is the *Iron Duke*, built in 1871 and withdrawn in May 1892 and right is No 3019 *Rover*, built in 1892 and withdrawn in 1908. Notice that the standard gauge locomotive's boiler is set higher in order to clear its 7ft 8½in diameter driving wheels. (Author's collection)

railways when each line was an entirety in itself, as the railway network grew, differing gauges prevented through running and it was found that unity of gauge was essential. Although the broad gauge had the edge on standard gauge, there were many more miles of standard gauge track in England and Wales as a whole and it was more economic to narrow a broad gauge line than to shift platforms and other line-side structures, widen bridges, cuttings and embankments. Sometimes a line was completely transformed to standard gauge while other broad gauge lines had a third rail added so that it could carry a train of either gauge. Usually a train was entirely of one gauge, but sometimes it contained rolling stock of two gauges. The very last broad gauge train ran on 21 May 1892. By that time the Great Western Railway had absorbed the Wilts, Somerset & Weymouth Railway and the Bristol & Exeter Railway on 14 March 1850 and 1 January 1876 respectively.

Dragon at Taunton heading the last broad gauge down 'Cornishman' on 20 May 1892. Notice the train shed, left. (Author's collection)

In addition to the principal railways mentioned there were two significant independent lines. The West Somerset Mineral Railway carried iron ore from the Brendon Hills down to Watchet where it was shipped to South Wales for smelting. The West Somerset Mineral Railway had no rail link with any other company. The Weston, Clevedon & Portishead Light Railway was set up to fill a need for a direct link between the three resorts, the existing Great Western line being far from a beeline – in fact its critics claimed that its initials stood for 'Great Way Round'. In addition to carrying passengers, the Weston, Clevedon & Portishead also carried coal from Wick St Lawrence Wharf to Clevedon gas works and stone from Black Rock quarry in the Gordano Valley to Portishead where it was carried onwards by the Great Western Railway.

Somerset also had several interesting industrial lines. There was the narrow gauge Oakhill Brewery railway carrying the firm's products to the Somerset & Dorset's Binegar station; the Kilmersdon colliery railway leading from the pit to the head of an incline where a descending loaded wagon hauled up an empty wagon. Pensford colliery also had an incline, but there a wagon was drawn up by a cable. There were, and still are, stone quarry railways in the eastern Mendips.

The 2ft 6in gauge *Mendip* at Oakhill Brewery *c* 1912. (Author's collection)

Although many of the branch lines were closed either immediately following or before the 1963 Beeching Report on Railways, some have re-opened as preserved lines: the West Somerset Railway, the East Somerset Railway and the Avon Valley Railway, while Network Rail has re-opened the Portishead branch as far as Portbury. Templecombe station had been re-opened to passengers and Worle Parkway built on a new site.

A significant amount of passenger and freight traffic in Somerset was transient, passing from east or north to the south-west. The main railway centre in the county was Taunton. Although lines did not all radiate from the town itself, they radiated from its environs to Exeter, Barnstaple, Minehead, Bristol, Castle Cary, Chard and Yeovil. Taunton's locomotive shed had the largest number of engines in Somerset and had an allocation of 57 on 31 December 1947, the eve of Nationalisation. Templecombe was another important junction for exchange traffic as the London & South Western Railway sent its traffic to the Midlands and North via the Somerset & Dorset Railway, while the Midland Railway despatched all its traffic to the South-West via the same route. Today there is no real rail centre in Somerset, Taunton being the closest as it is the junction of routes from Exeter, Bristol and Castle Cary. Express trains still terminate at Weston super Mare and until the growth of the private car ownership brought them to a halt, holiday trains terminated at Minehead. Coal from the Radstock area formed the heaviest traffic originating in Somerset, other important items being stone, agricultural products – particularly milk – and manufactured goods. Today it is stone from Hapsford and Whatley, cars and coal from Portbury and atomic waste from Bridgwater.

3 How a Railway was Created

IN THE 19th century businessmen and landowners wishing to improve trade, increase the value of their property and invest their cash profitably might propose a scheme for linking two places by a railway. The way they went about such a scheme followed a general pattern which can be described once and serve to tell the story of the creation of almost any railway in Somerset. Several meetings would be called in the locality and provided that sufficient financial support was promised, a bill would be placed before Parliament, itself often

proving an expensive process. Committees of the houses of Commons and Lords received evidence for and against the proposed line. If both houses passed the bill it became an Act of Parliament and the promoting company was then legally entitled to raise a stipulated sum of money to purchase land and build the railway between the two chosen places. Before going to Parliament a surveyor would have drawn up plans. Ideally, a line would be straight, level, and pass through or close to chief settlements, yet using cheaper, rather than expensive land. If tunnels, cuttings and embankments were required, the surveyor would endeavour to make sure that soil excavated could be used in a nearby embankment. Those plans, known as Deposited Plans, were placed with the local authority and Parliament. After the passing of the Act and the capital raised, a contractor had to be found to carry out the work; those companies with less money would seek one willing to work for shares rather than for cash.

Work usually began with the ceremonial turning of the first turf, a highly decorated spade being used to lift the sod into an equally ornate wheelbarrow. That was often done by the company's chairman or his wife. After the ceremony the directors and local dignitaries dined. The contractor set to work and was likely to meet difficulties – a shortage of workers or materials, hard rock in an unexpected place that had to be cut through, or fluid clay that refused to stay in place. The railway company might be unable to raise enough money to pay the contractor or the contractor himself might go bankrupt. Parliament wisely decided that a railway company must deposit a sum of money so that in the event of failure to complete the line after work had started the money deposited could be used to re-instate the property purchased

The highly ornate wheelbarrow and spade used by Mrs Milward. (Author's collection)

compulsorily from the landowners. The Act of Parliament stipulated that a line should be completed within a certain period of time and quite often, because of various difficulties, the railway was forced to apply to Parliament for an extension of time and not infrequently for an increase in capital to cover unforeseen costs.

When the contractor completed the line and before it could be opened to passenger traffic, an inspection had to be undertaken for the Board of Trade through an officer of the Royal Engineers. He went over the line testing bridges and other structures, making sure that the signalling was adequate for safety and the stations had suitable facilities. Usually at least one fault was discovered. If it was minor the Board of Trade granted a certificate subject to its correction; if there was major criticism, re-inspection was required before the line could be opened.

On the opening day the directors and local dignitaries travelled over the line, dining afterwards. If the railway was a local one, it was usually worked by a larger company to make the business more economic. That was because, although perhaps the line might require only one engine and two passenger coaches to work services, at least one more engine would be needed as a spare when the other engine was having a boiler wash-out or undergoing repair. On market days, fair days and Bank Holidays two coaches might prove insufficient. Some goods traffic required special rolling stock and it would not be sensible to invest capital in something used only occasionally. To obviate such difficulties a small company therefore usually arranged for a larger company with larger resources to work the line for a percentage of the gross receipts. Some lines were far from profitable, ordinary shareholders rarely or never receiving a dividend, and it often happened that eventually a small railway was purchased by the working company, the payment usually less than its building cost.

Particularly if it was a branch line, it probably suffered from bus competition in the 1920s, buses being more convenient as passengers could board nearer their homes and be dropped nearer their destinations. Railway stations tended to be built at locations convenient from the railway's point of view, quite often some distance from a village or town centre. To help combat bus competition, unstaffed halts were opened at points near to centres of population.

Railmotor No 75 on 27 May 1925. This was a combined locomotive and coach. The vertical boiler is behind the third and fourth windows from the right, with the chimney poking through the roof. The driver controlled the vehicle from either end. (Author's collection)

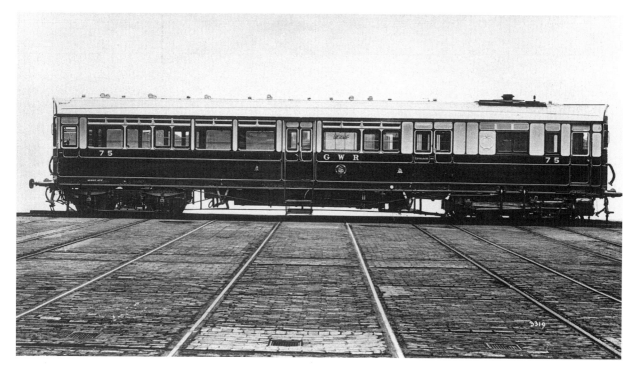

In the early 1900s railmotors came into use. A railmotor was a passenger coach and locomotive contained on the same underframe. It was designed so that when going boiler-first the engine would be at the front but when returning the driver could walk to what had been the rear and drive from a special control compartment, the fireman remaining at the other end. The use of a railmotor obviated the time and trouble needed to run an engine round its train at the end of every journey. When a railmotor service was introduced, unmanned halts were opened at places where traffic was insufficient to warrant a staffed station.

Railmotors were found to lack flexibility. If, on (say) a market day, the number of passengers quadrupled, a railmotor could not cope as it was only powerful enough to draw one trailer. As a railway had to have a locomotive and coaches standing by for such an eventuality, then any saving made by the railmotor was lost.

The solution was a push-pull or auto train. An engine stayed at one end of the train and on the return journey the driver could control his engine from a special compartment at what had been the rear by means of mechanical rods or compressed air.

The year 1923 brought Grouping when, apart from very minor lines, all railway companies became part of one of the Big Four: the Great Western Railway (GWR), the London, Midland & Scottish Railway (LMS); the London & North Eastern Railway (LNER) and the Southern Railway (SR). The GWR was the only railway to retain its old name, the London & South Western Railway becoming part of the SR and the Midland Railway part of the LMS. The Weston, Clevedon & Portishead Light Railway was unaffected by Grouping and the Somerset & Dorset Joint Railway continued to be run as a joint line but its owners changed from the Midland Railway and the London & South Western Railway to the LMS and SR. With Nationalisation on 1 January 1948 the GWR became British Railways, Western Region, and the SR the Southern Region, though minor area changes were made.

Railways were quick to spot the bus competitor and themselves participated in road transport, the GWR owning its first bus in 1903 though its first service in Somerset, between Bridgwater and Stogursey, was not inaugurated until 11 April 1906. The London & South Western Railway operated several bus routes, but none within Somerset.

0-4-2T No 1463 pushes the 11.00am Clevedon to Yatton past Kingston Bridge on 13 June 1957. The driver controls the engine from a special compartment at the front of the leading coach. (Author)

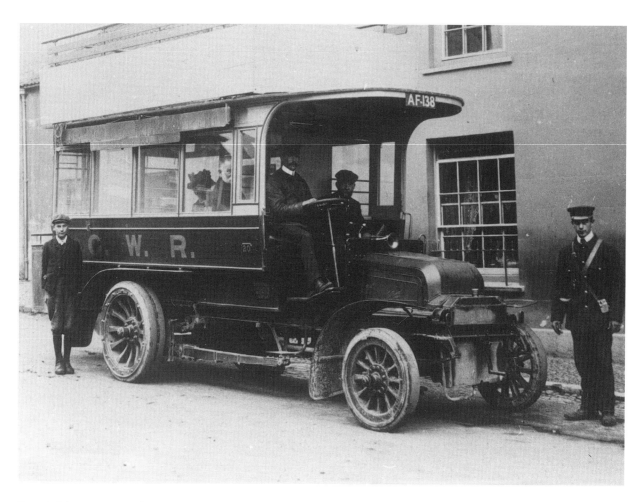

From 1 July 1908 until 31 October 1908 the Great Western Railway ran a bus service from Bridgwater to Holford and Kilve to serve the area north of the Minehead branch. The service was not a success. Here Driver Hancock is at the wheel of a 20hp Milnes-Daimler, registration AF 138, fleet number 20. The conductor with cash bag and ticket punch stands to the right. (Author's collection)

From 1928 legislation permitted railways to purchase large, but not controlling, shareholdings in existing bus companies. The GWR and SR reached agreement with the National Omnibus & Transport Company: the Western National was set up to run bus services in GWR territory, the railway agreeing to transfer its road motor services to that company in return for a half share, the Western National undertaking to co-ordinate rail and road services and not to compete with the railway. The Southern National operated similar services in the SR area, which in Somerset comprised the district around Yeovil. From 1 January 1929 the GWR also owned shares in the Bristol Tramways & Carriage Company. On 22 July 1931 the GWR bus services at Portishead and Weston super Mare passed into BTCC hands.

In addition to bus competition, the increase in private car ownership in the 1950s and the 1960s was another reason for the decline in the number of rail passengers and many of the poorly-frequented stations closed. The smaller stations remaining open were generally unstaffed, passengers purchasing their tickets from the conductor-guard on the diesel multiple unit pay trains. Freight traffic also declined because of increased use of road vehicles, especially at times when railwaymen were on strike, their actions permanently damaging business. The swing to the use of electricity, North Sea gas and oil for heating brought a decrease in the once very heavy coal traffic to almost every station. Forty-five years ago railways carried relatively small loads to a variety of destinations; today the railways are the only bulk carriers of stone, steel, cars, coal and oil.

4 Broad Gauge Lines: The Great Western Railway

IN THE early 19th century Bristol was the second city in the kingdom and needed a quicker and safer method of transport than road or canal. One of the protagonists in the struggle for improvement, a Bristol wine merchant, complained that beer and spirits conveyed by canal were frequently pilfered or adulterated *en route*, a favourite practice being the unlawful abstraction of a portion of the contents of a vessel and its replacement with water. A Bath draper declared that he experienced a depreciation of 20% in goods owing to the change of fashion while they were in transit by barge.

The 118½ miles of the GWR from London to Bristol was opened in stages, the first at the London end being ready in 1838; the Bristol to Bath section was

Bathford Halt, view up, 23 May 1963. When opened on 18 March 1929 the halt was a timber structure. That was replaced by concrete components cast at the Taunton Concrete Depot. (Author)

(Left) At Bathampton, a Portsmouth train curves away from the Swindon line on 22 May 1959. (Author)

(Right) Broad gauge 2-4-0 No 14 heads an up express west of Bathampton *c* 1890. Notice the mixed gauge track on the main line, but the siding to the right is just standard gauge. (Author's collection)

completed on 31 August 1840 and the final section from Chippenham to Bath, including Box Tunnel, on 31 May 1841.

The first GWR station to be reached after crossing the Somerset border from Wiltshire was Bathford Halt, opened on 18 March 1929 at a cost of approximately £164. It closed on 4 January 1965. To the east were Farleigh Down Quarry sidings, opened in 1882, closed in 1930, but re-opened in 1937 for Air Ministry ammunition storage. The sidings eventually closed in 1950. One resourceful signalman there made a 20-ft rod so that he could fish from his signal box.

The Wilts, Somerset & Weymouth Railway joined the GWR immediately east of Bathampton station, which closed on 3 October 1966. From 1920 Bathampton forwarded about 2 tons of paper daily in small consignments. Hampton Row Halt had a short life, opening on 18 March 1907 and closing, as a wartime economy measure, on 25 April 1917. Beyond the site of the halt the line passes through Sydney Gardens and adds, rather than detracts, from the park's pleasantness. The balustraded stone wall there forms an unusual, if not unique, railway boundary. As Bath station was in such a decrepit condition when Princess Helena visited the city on 13 June 1889, a temporary platform was built for her in Sydney Gardens.

Bath station was approached over the 255yd Dolemeads Viaduct and in

Diesel-hydraulic No 1027 *Western Lancer* heads an up express to Paddington through Sydney Gardens, Bath, on 28 April 1970. Notice the balustrade forming an unusual railway boundary. (Revd Alan Newman)

1855 a school was built partly beneath one of the archways. An adjoining arch provided a covered playground. Bath Spa station, a Grade II listed building, is set between two bridges only 700ft apart, and in addition to passenger facilities a goods depot and an engine shed were also squeezed into the site. The station itself is on a 20-arch viaduct. The style of the building is Elizabethan and the bridges between Bath and Bristol continue that style and use a pointed Tudor arch design. The original train shed lasted until 1897. In 1895 the station was lit by electricity, one of the first in England to have that form of illumination. Prince, the last shunting horse at the station, retired in 1959. At Bath, as at all the principal GWR stations, second-class passengers were not allowed to come into contact with those travelling first class. In June 1842 pens were provided

Bath station was in such a poor state of repair that it was totally unfit to receive Princess Helena on 13 June 1889. Just for her benefit a temporary station was built in Sydney Gardens to serve the up line. Here the princess is leaving the train. (Author's collection)

Bath station *c* 1845, view towards Swindon. Unfortunately the pillars supporting the train shed were placed so near the edge of the platform that detraining passengers bumped into them. (J C Bourne)

for first- and second-class passengers, those of the former class having the luxury of a waiting room adjoining their pen. There were also separate exits from the platforms. Third-class passengers used the goods station.

No smoking was allowed on GWR premises, any infringement being reported to the directors as the Minute of 14 October 1840 shows:

> *The circumstances attending the case of the two first class passengers having on the 9th instant smoked cigars at Bath station, where they were remonstrated with by the [railway] police sergeant, who showed them the Bye-laws of the Company and one of whom afterwards resumed smoking in the carriage between Bath and Keynsham, was reported to the Committee by the Secretary who had been directed to take steps for the infliction of the penalty. Having presented a letter from the offending parties strongly expressive of their contrition, it was ordered that further proceedings should be stayed on their paying the amount of the fine incurred – forty shillings – to be appropriated in donations of £1 each, to the Bristol Infirmary and to the General Hospital, with an announcement of the same to the public, in each of the Bristol newspapers.*

With the opening of the station in 1840 Moses Pickwick (whose name inspired Dickens) organised a horse omnibus to meet every train, the round trip starting and ending at his White Hart Inn. Dorchester Street and Manvers Street had been built by the GWR to give access to its station. Half of Dorchester Street had previously been built but Manvers Street was new and had to be kept in

Dismantling the bridge linking Bath station with the Royal Hotel, 1936. (Author's collection)

repair by the GWR until two-thirds of it was lined with buildings. Responsibility then fell on the landowner, Lord Manvers.

Until 26 January 1936 an interesting feature of the station was a footbridge from the up platform directly into the Royal Hotel on the opposite side of the road. Another interesting peculiarity was the signal box perched on the awning of the down platform. It was sited in that odd position the give the signalman a clear view in both directions on a fairly sharp curve. One of the first left-luggage offices was opened at Bath in 1846 but although it seemed successful the GWR ordered it to be closed after only one week's use.

An excursion train carrying passengers to the Great Exhibition of 1851 caused problems at Bath. It was scheduled to leave at 6.30am and people arrived at 5.30am. Shortly after 6 o'clock the booking hall was full and hundreds of potential passengers crowded outside. Three open goods trucks were attached to the train to increase the accommodation. As many as 1600 managed to travel on that train to London, twice the number of the previous largest excursion from Bath, but 200 had to be turned away disappointed. One excursion from Bristol that year consisted of 1700 people in 30 coaches drawn by no less than three engines.

Spanning the Avon west of the station was a laminated timber bridge, the most oblique ever built of wood. Bank to bank the canalised river was 80ft wide but the bridge spanned 164ft. It was replaced by an iron structure in 1878.

The viaduct west of the station contained a police station. It closed in April 1923 and the premises were taken over by a greengrocer. A nearby arch was the city mortuary. Westmoreland Road goods depot opened in 1877 to replace the cramped shed adjacent to the passenger station. Apart from other traffic, the depot was used for the despatch of cranes from Stothert & Pitt's works on the opposite side of the road, but the works were also served directly by the rival

The skew bridge over the Avon west of Bath c 1845. Notice the crossbar signal on the left of the bridge. (J C Bourne)

The mortuary at Bath set in a railway arch, 12 October 1963. The scroll above the doorway reads: 'BUSA' for Bath Union Sanitary Authority. (Author)

The interior of Hospital Train No 21 which passed through Bath during World War I. Ward D is in the foreground and Wards E and F beyond. Lighting is by gas. Notice the D-shaped hand grip to help a patient get up. (Author's collection)

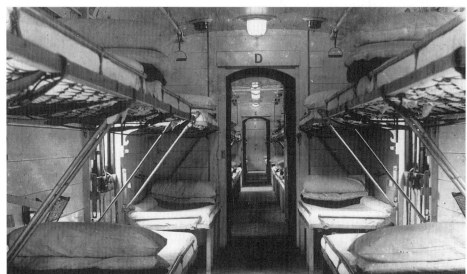

Westgate Street, Bath, c 1947. Two methods of GWR road delivery: a Scarab mechanical horse and trailer, left; Charlie Hooper and his horse-drawn van, right. (Author's collection)

LMS line. A small engine shed for the GWR Bath shunting engine was concealed beneath a large water tank. Part of the Westmoreland yard is now used as a transfer depot for containers carrying refuse from Bath to Calvert in Buckinghamshire.

Oldfield Park Platform – 'platform' was a manned halt – opened on 18 February 1929 to serve a developing suburb. It is used by about 500 passengers daily and is particularly useful for people from the area travelling to Bristol, as the competing bus services are north of the river and therefore not easily accessible.

Twerton Viaduct built as cottages to gain income for the expenditure. They were never occupied as dwellings as a result of smoke problems because part of the chimney ran parallel with the ground. Diesel railcars Nos 35 and 36 with an intermediate trailer are working the 8.05am Bristol Temple Meads to Weymouth on 20 April 1954. (Author)

Twerton station, a Grade II three-story building in Tudor style, closed on 2 April 1917 as a wartime economy measure and never re-opened. Part of Twerton Viaduct, also Grade II listed, was intended to be let out as two-roomed homes. It is believed that they were never occupied for that purpose, probably because the flues ran parallel to the floor. A fire was then essential both for cooking and heating and smoke did not readily find its way to the chimneys.

Nearby the railway ran through the grounds of Twerton Vicarage. Unfortunately, before the incumbent and his family could move into a replacement home built for them by the GWR, navvies cut through the drains of the house causing an outbreak of typhoid which resulted in the death of the vicar's son.

The line passed through the two Twerton tunnels, 45yd and 264yd in length, both with very attractive Tudor-Gothic arches with flanking towers, all four portals Grade II listed. When Newton Cutting was made a Roman villa was unearthed and the mosaic pavement depicting Orpheus and his lute is now in Bristol City Museum.

Saltford station opened on 16 December 1840 and was particularly busy when Saltford Regatta was held. Some passengers used it when going to Bath Races at Lansdown. The station closed on 5 January 1970. Beyond is Saltford Tunnel, 176yd in length. Saltford

A 'Hall' class locomotive heads a down Portsmouth to Cardiff train west of Twerton Tunnel *c* 1960. (K Hampton)

was supplied with water from springs having their origin in the hill south-west of the village, but the navvies cut across the springs, stopping the supply. For several years the GWR was required to deliver water by cart to the inhabitants, the cart bearing a notice stating that the company was bound to provide a water supply as it had stopped the original source.

Keynsham station is still open but the Tudor-style buildings were demolished in 1970. Following the opening of Fry's chocolate factory, from 1 February 1925 the station was renamed Keynsham & Somerdale. The platforms had to be almost doubled in length to cope with Fry's workers' trains and also excursion trains carrying visitors to the factory. Between 1925 and 1980 the factory was served by a private siding and the vans that brought the ingredients were used

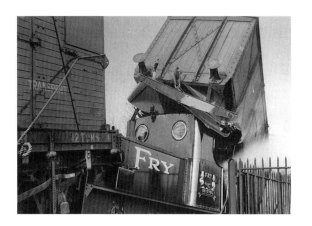

for the despatch of the final product to Fry's distribution depots and elsewhere. A main-line engine shunted vans in and out, but for other movements within the factory grounds from 1928 until 1964 Fry's had their own vertical boiler Sentinel locomotive. From 1956 they also used a Hudswell Clarke

0-4-0 diesel-mechanical. Messrs E S & A Robinson, paper manufacturers, had an Avonside geared 0-4-0 that started on petrol and then changed over to the cheaper paraffin. Two short-term owners of private sidings were Square Grip Reinforcement Co (London) Limited from 1955 to 1966, and Tate & Lyle between 1952 and 1966. Keynsham goods depot was used by Polysulphin, manufacturers of industrial soaps, and Gould Thomas, chemical manufacturers.

West of Keynsham Hams water troughs were installed, allowing engines to replenish their supply. The line passes through the Grade II -listed Fox's Wood Tunnel (1017yd), so named, not after the animal but from Dr Edward Fox, a Quaker who believed in humane treatment for the insane and had brass bands playing on the lawns of Brislington House for the entertainment of the inmates. The GWR had a quarry at Fox's Wood and for safety reasons blasting operations at the quarry could only be carried out with the sanction of the signalman at Fox's Wood box. A brass 'Blasting disc for Fox's Wood Quarry' was kept in the box and given to the quarry assistant foremen as permission to blast, the signalman then sending an 'Obstruction Danger' signal to boxes on either side and not allowing them to forward trains.

Between Fox's Wood Tunnel and the 154yd St Anne's Tunnel the line runs picturesquely beside the Avon and close to Birchwood Quarry. On 31 March 1876 John Chiddy, quarry foreman, noticed a large stone which had fallen and fouled the down line. Knowing that the prestigious 'Flying Dutchman' was imminent he struggled to shift the obstruction. He succeeded in moving it clear of the track but he himself was unable to step clear of the express and was killed. Had he not moved the stone the train would have been derailed into the river with great loss of life.

The train stopped and a collection was made for his widow and seven children. How much did those grateful passengers donate? A total of £3 17s 0d. Lord Elcho was so incensed at the poor response that he took the case to Parliament and asserted that if a man risked his life to save others he should do so 'with the consciousness that his family would not be dependent on charity or the workhouse'. The Chancellor of the Exchequer explained that no government funds were available to help such people.

The press publicity resulted in an account being opened in Bristol and another in Bath. The Bank of England contributed £10 when informed that two of its officials had been on the train with a large quantity of bullion. A total of £400 was collected and with that sum a

No 6023 *King Edward II* picks up water at Keynsham troughs on 11 June 1957. The storage tank, to replenish the troughs set between the running rails, can be seen on the left. In British Railways days the 'Great', on a Great Western cast iron notice, such as that seen lower right, was painted out to make it more appropriate. (Author)

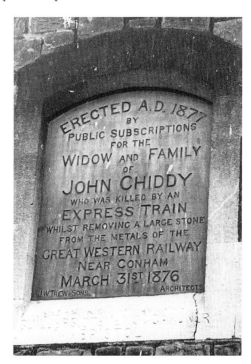

Plaque on the wall of Memorial Cottage. (Author)

The original position of Fox's Wood troughs from 27 June 1896 until 30 October 1898. The Avon is on the right and it is here that the train would have been derailed had not John Chiddy removed the rock. Notice the permanent way hut to the right of the line. (Author's collection)

Demolishing Bristol No 1 Tunnel, 1887. Notice the steam crane high on the right and a railway wagon – presumably with a coal supply. It is interesting to contemplate how they were raised into such a position. (Author's collection)

cottage and smallholding were bought on the opposite side of the river in Gloucestershire. The house, Memorial Cottage, stands in what is now Memorial Road.

By the east portal of St Anne's Tunnel was St Anne's Pumping Station that supplied water to the two Bristol locomotive depots. During World War II a bomb destroyed the filter, so water was pumped direct from the river and an eel spent three years in the water tank of a shunting engine fed by its crew. Beyond the west portal of the tunnel was St Anne's Park station, opened on 23 May 1898 to serve a growing suburb. It closed on 5 January 1970 and has since been demolished. Beyond was Bristol No 1 Tunnel, opened out in 1889 and widened to form a vertical-sided cutting. The line then leaves Somerset.

The Bristol & North Somerset Railway

Not far beyond the erstwhile Bristol No 1 Tunnel is North Somerset Junction where the single track Bristol & North Somerset Railway ran to Radstock, tapping collieries *en route*. Although the first turf was turned on 7 October 1863, the company ran into financial difficulties and its image was further tarnished when its secretary was sentenced to 12 months' imprisonment with hard labour for attempting to defraud a Bristol banker. The line eventually opened on 18 June 1874. Although closed to passengers on 2 November 1959, the profitable goods and mineral traffic continued until part of the line was washed away on 10 July 1968 and it was deemed uneconomic to repair.

2-6-2T No 4536 crosses Pensford Viaduct with a Bristol to Frome train, 1 September 1953. (Author)

Brislington station, one of William Clarke's standard designs, was a typical village station yet set in a city suburb. The line climbed to Whitchurch Halt, opened on 1 January 1925. Pensford station building was similar to that at Brislington and beyond it is the still extant 995-ft, 16-arch Grade II-listed viaduct. On the other side were the sidings for Pensford Colliery. The pit was situated about 100ft above the level of the GWR and a stationary engine hauled wagons up the incline. From the foot of the incline a loaded wagon ran by gravity to the departure sidings while an empty wagon gravitated from another siding to the foot of the incline, ready to be hauled up. The last load left the colliery on 13 December 1958.

From Pensford Colliery a 2-ft gauge tramway ran to Bromley Colliery, about a mile distant. Bromley had been opened in the latter half of the 19th century and in 1909 was bought by the company that was to open the pit at Pensford. That company built the tramway across the fields using embankments and cuttings to give access to Pensford Colliery and the GWR. Initially, that narrow-gauge line was worked by an Avonside 0-4-0T but it was found to be underpowered and prone to derailment. It was sold in 1913 and was replaced by main and tail rope haulage, the cable running over rollers in the centre of the track and returning by the side. It was capable of moving about 50 tubs at a time, each tub holding 7½ cwt of coal. It was the last pit in Somerset to use pit ponies and closed on 18 May 1957.

John Royale Williams, station master at Brislington, stands proudly by his coronation flower bed, 1911. (Author's collection)

(Left) From Bromley Sidings, Pensford, an empty coal wagon is being drawn up to the colliery on 8 September 1953. Loaded wagons stand in the siding in the right background. (Author)

(Right) Skips on the 2ft gauge tramway linking Bromley Colliery with Pensford Colliery, 23 August 1956. The rope returns on the left hand side of the track. (Author)

An unusual accident occurred at Chelwood Bridge about 1944. An American Army lorry dislodged a coping stone that fell on the firebox of a locomotive unfortunately passing below. Steam escaped from the damaged firebox and scalded the crew. The Pensford signalwoman saw escaping steam, rightly realised that the engine was out of control, quickly pulled off the signals and in due course allowed the train to halt on the rising gradient beyond.

Before reaching Clutton station more collieries were tapped; one siding about ¾ mile in length served Greyfield Colliery. Initially this was gravity-worked with horses drawing empties up to the pit but latterly an engine was employed. Hallatrow was the junction of the line to Limpley Stoke described on page 36. Among other traffic, Hallatrow dealt with the output of the Purnell printing works and there was also a quarry siding. Farrington Gurney Halt, opened on 11 July 1927, was famous for the fact that passengers boarding there were required to buy their tickets at the Miners' Arms public house. North of the halt were sidings serving Farrington and Springfield collieries. The former opened in 1882 with horse traction but was later worked by various small locomotives until closure in 1921. The Springfield line was worked by horses until 1940 when a Ruston & Hornsby 4-wheel diesel-mechanical shunter was brought into use and remained until closure in 1966.

More collieries were passed before Midsomer Norton & Welton station. Beyond, the line ran parallel with the Somerset & Dorset Railway, but at a lower

Clutton station *c* 1910; lighting is by oil. Hanging from the palings is a device known as a 'skid' for rolling barrels to and from a road vehicle. (M J Tozer collection)

Greyfield Colliery near Clutton *c* 1905. The 0-4-0ST colliery shunter is either *Francis* or *Daisy*. The wagons have solid wooden buffers that were banned from main line railways after 31 December 1914 but could continue to be used within collieries. (Author's collection)

0-6-0PT No 9612 approaches Clutton with a Bristol to Frome train on 11 September 1953. On the embankment, right, is the formation to the erstwhile Fry's Bottom Colliery. (Author)

Passengers from Farrington Gurney Halt purchased tickets from the ticket office at the Miners' Arms. This view was taken in September 1936. (Author's collection)

2-6-2T No 4551
leaves Midsomer
Norton & Welton
station with the
4.28pm Frome to
Bristol Temple
Meads on 6 July
1955. (Revd Alan
Newman)

2-6-2PT No 4131
arrives at Radstock
West from Bristol
with empty coal
wagons on 14
August 1959. The
station building is a
typical William
Clarke design. The
signalman is
climbing the steps
after collecting the
single line tablet
from the fireman.
(Author)

0-6-2PT No 7772 at
Radstock West
having its tanks
replenished by a
water crane before
returning to Bristol,
12 April 1961.
(Author)

The signalman at Radstock West holds his hand to receive the single line tablet from the fireman on No 5757 working a Bristol to Frome passenger train. It is 1953, the year of Queen Elizabeth's coronation, and bunting may be seen on buildings in the background. (Author's collection)

0-6-0PT No 9681 on 6 March 1999 hauling a London & North Western Railway van built in 1916. It is on the North Somerset Heritage Trust line that hopes to re-open between Radstock and Frome. (Author)

level. Although the Bristol & North Somerset Railway terminated at Radstock, the line continued as part of the Wilts, Somerset & Weymouth Railway (Chapter 6). Radstock West signal box is now preserved at the Didcot Railway Centre. When the Somerset & Dorset Railway closed on 7 March 1966 a chord line was constructed to form a link with the former Bristol and North Somerset Railway to enable coal to be removed from Writhlington Colliery. That pit remained open until 1973.

Hallatrow to Limpley Stoke

The branch from Hallatrow to Limpley Stoke has a fascinating history. It started as a Bristol & North Somerset Railway branch from Hallatrow down to Camerton and opened to passengers and goods on 1 March 1882, worked by the GWR and taken over by that company when it absorbed the Bristol & North Somerset on 1 July 1884. Principal traffic on the branch was coal and it was most unfortunate that loaded trains faced a rising gradient of 1 in 47. Furthermore, curves increased friction and limited coal trains to a maximum of 15 wagons. A solitary passenger coach sufficed and one train each way daily was coupled to goods wagons rather than run as a separate service. Until that branch

was opened, most of Camerton's coal had been removed along the Somerset Coal Canal but following the line's inauguration, coal traffic was insufficient to cover the cost of maintaining the waterway. It closed in 1898.

In 1903 the moribund Somerset Coal Canal was sold to the GWR for £2000 and was used for part of a new line built from Camerton to a junction with the former Wilts, Somerset & Weymouth Railway near Limpley Stoke, *en route* tapping at Dunkerton, the largest colliery in Somerset. That new line had a ruling gradient of 1 in 100 and moreover it was in favour of loaded trains. Although designed to cope with trains of 50 wagons, in the event it is believed that no train of that length ever used the branch.

The line was extended from Camerton to Dunkerton Colliery on 26 August 1907, coal trains still having to climb the 1 in 47 from Camerton to Hallatrow until the line was opened through Limpley Stoke. The 7-mile section from Dunkerton to Limpley Stoke included a 78yd viaduct at Dunkerton and three more viaducts at Midford, totalling a further 153yd. The 66yd tunnel at Combe Hay was the old canal tunnel adapted for railway use, while a footbridge cast at Paulton in 1811 spanning the canal at Monkton Combe was raised and enabled pedestrians to cross the railway.

(Left) The Camerton branch was built partly along the bed of the Somerset Coal Canal. Here, west of Monkton Combe, we see the divergence: the Somerset Coal Canal was in the dip in the foreground. This view was taken on 18 April 1952. (Author)

(Right) The footbridge over the Somerset Coal Canal at Monkton Combe *c* 1900. It bore an inscription 'Cast at Paulton 1811'. (Courtesy Monkton Combe School)

Loaded wagon sidings at Dunkerton Colliery, view west *c* 1910. The Camerton branch is on the far right. (Author's collection)

Constructing the
Camerton to
Limpley Stoke line
west of Midford
Viaduct *c* 1909.
Notice the steam
excavator at the end
of the cutting.
(Author's collection)

The line opened to passengers and goods on 9 May 1910. Initially, the five trains each way from Hallatrow to Limpley Stoke were worked by a locomotive and auto coach, but at an early date the service was worked by a third-class-only steam rail motor stabled overnight at Radstock. The passenger service was withdrawn on 22 March 1915 as a wartime economy measure. Following local pressure the service was reinstated on 9 July 1923 but withdrawn on 21 September 1925 as uneconomic. The problem was that the line ran east to west, whereas passenger movements were mostly north and south, to Bath or Radstock respectively. Certainly, on at least one occasion after the line had been closed to regular passenger trains, Monkton Combe School chartered a rail motor to transport scholars to Saltford Regatta. That may have been the occasion when an 'eight' was also carried by rail. As it overhung one wagon, a

The west portal of
Combe Hay Tunnel
on 20 July 1952,
formerly used by the
Somerset Coal
Canal. (Author)

second was used and was firmly lashed to both. Imagine what happened when the first curve was traversed!

Three or four coal trains plus a general goods train ran daily until Dunkerton Colliery closed on 6 September 1927, after which one train sufficed. Had Dunkerton Colliery been worked with foresight rather than a mad rush to mine as much coal as easily as possible, it would have remained open longer. Withdrawal of passenger services rendered the section from Hallatrow to Camerton redundant and it was closed on 8 February 1932. Camerton Colliery closed in 1950 and after that date trains on the branch averaged less than one a month. The very last goods train ran on 14 February 1951.

Originally Hallatrow had a single platform but a bay platform was added for the Camerton branch passenger trains. In preparation for the extension to Limpley Stoke an up platform was added and the existing platform, which became the down, was extended. The cost of the expansion, including engineering and signalling, came to £8790 – a significant sum in 1910.

Paulton Halt opened on 5 January 1914 and had a very short life before being closed with the withdrawal of the passenger service on 22 March 1915. Probably shelterless, it was constructed of stone with a brick facing. As it was some distance from habitation it was very lightly used.

Radford & Timsbury Halt had a slightly longer life as it was opened with the extension through to Limpley Stoke. The timber platform had a corrugated-iron pagoda shelter. From about 1900 a siding served Lower Conygre Colliery, but following the closure of that pit in 1916 the siding continued to be used for the output of Priston Colliery until about 1925.

Camerton had a single platform and a William Clarke building. The station had one of the three signal boxes on the branch. All were the GWR brick-built design of the period. Beyond was a line up to the colliery.

Dunkerton Colliery Halt opened on 9 October 1911 with a corrugated-iron pagoda shelter; its total cost was £230. It was principally for colliery workers as villagers of Carlingcott and Tunley faced a steep climb. Adjacent was a brick-

An auto train hauled by a 0-4-2T enters Radford & Timsbury Halt *c* 1910. The lady wears a conspicuous hat well decorated with flowers. (Author's collection)

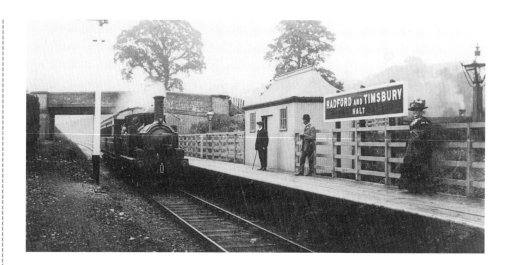

Camerton station *c* 1910, a typical William Clarke design. The number of milk churns indicates good traffic in that commodity. Four staff stand on the platform and to the left of the station building is the oil store. GWR posters advertise the 'Holiday Haunts' book and excursion trains. An enamel sign reads: 'Good morning with Pears' soap'. The coal wagons in the foreground are local: Timsbury Colliery, Camerton Colliery and Charles Skeates, coal merchant, Bath. (Author's collection)

built overline bridge to an unusual design because of the line's location on the side of a hill. A footpath on railway property was built to the pit at a cost of £60, half of the sum being defrayed by the colliery owners.

Dunkerton Colliery sidings were quite extensive and their entrance controlled by a signal box. At the Camerton end of the ½-mile site were three looped sidings for storing empty wagons; there were six lines serving the loading screens. At the Limpley Stoke end of the complex were four looped sidings for loaded wagons. The sidings were shunted by a Peckett 0-4-0ST. During World War II a train of about six ambulance coaches was stored there, an engine moving them periodically to prevent the bearings from seizing. In the post-war period the sidings were used for storing wagons awaiting repair.

Between the colliery and Dunkerton station the line crossed Dunkerton Viaduct. Dunkerton station consisted of a wooden frame on a brick plinth, the walls panelled with 3ft-square artificial stone slabs. The station had the branch's third signal box. As at Camerton, although two trains could cross, because only one platform was provided, it was not possible to cross two passenger trains, only one passenger and one goods, or two goods.

Camerton station on 18 July 1952 following closure of the branch. (Author)

On the Limpley Stoke side of Combe Hay Tunnel was Combe Hay Halt with a brick-faced platform surmounted by a shelter. When opened, a farmer complained that the approach path was too narrow to admit a trolley, which meant that all heavy luggage and milk churns had to be manhandled to the platform. The problem was never overcome.

One hot summer's day, as a permanent way trolley approached Combe Hay Tunnel, the gangers on board were surprised to see that the rails inside had vanished. Closer inspection revealed that they were, indeed, still there but covered with sheep that had squeezed through a fence and found the tunnel a cool and shady place to rest.

A porter at Camerton frequented dances at Combe Hay. As he knew where the key of the hand-propelled permanent way trolley was hidden, he used this

Arthur Gerrish is seated on a manually-propelled 'dolly' at Monkton Combe West Ground Frame, 1946. Bert Gane is in the background. (M Halbrook collection)

Arthur Gerrish, left, and Gilbert Drew, right, on a manually-operated 'pump' trolley which had to be worked in a standing position. Notice the brake pedal between the two wheels. (M Drew collection)

method of transport. On arrival he locked the trolley securely to the rails and after the dance used it for his return journey.

Permanent way men were adept at using natural resources. Between Combe Hay and Midford large filberts grew beside the line and the men would go home with their hats full. Blackberries and mushrooms could be gathered from nearby fields and rabbit snares could be set on embankments.

Each Monday morning the ganger setting out to check the line made sure that he had a sackful of wooden keys to wedge the running rails in the chairs. That was because at weekends, if the weather was cold, miners kicked the keys out and used them on fires that they lit in permanent way huts set beside the line every 1½ miles. The permanent way men left the huts unlocked because they discovered that if secured, the miners always broke the doors open. Inside they upended a bucket, threw a newspaper over it and played cards.

As Midford Halt was on an embankment it was timber-built for lightness. With the corrugated-iron pagoda it cost £403 and opened on 27 February 1911. Unlike the other stations and halts on the line it did not re-open after the First World War. One Midford resident recalled that only one or two passengers used it each week. As a lad he made only one trip on the line. That was when he travelled by steam railmotor to Combe Hay Halt and then drove a pig back along the lanes.

The station building at Monkton Combe was a mirror-image of that at Dunkerton. There was a goods loop and flock mill siding. Mill Lane crossing was at one end of the station and in order not to block road traffic when a long goods train was expected, it was the practice to stop short and divide the train. At the beginning and end of term Monkton Combe School used the railway, and a private lorry, cheaper than hiring one from the GWR, conveyed luggage to and from the station. Usually three vans were loaded with trunks, tuck boxes and bicycles. At such times an extra porter was sent from Bath to assist with the traffic, one booking and the other attaching labels.

The main Bathampton to Westbury line was reached about half a mile before Limpley Stoke station, where the actual junction was. That design allowed through running to the east as coal from the Cam Valley collieries was destined for ships' bunkers at Southampton. In preparation for the opening of the branch the main line platforms at Limpley Stoke were extended by 200ft and the down platform lengthened by a further 150ft to provide a bay for the steam railmotors. A new building was provided on the down platform constructed in a similar fashion to those at Dunkerton and Monkton Combe. It is believed that some fittings from the original building, notably the doors and windows, were re-used. Exchange sidings for storing empty and loaded wagons were provided each side of the main line between Limpley Stoke and Freshford.

The Camerton branch proved quite popular with film producers. In 1931 *The Ghost Train* by Bath author Arnold Ridley was shot at Camerton, and publicity folders were distributed to cinema audiences. When shown at London cinemas most of the picture-house vestibules were converted to replica GWR booking halls – all good publicity for the company. The actual filming itself proved a very great attraction and as many as 5000 travelled from Bath and Bristol to watch proceedings, many staying through the night as some scenes were shot after dark. On 21 June 1931 a train of six corridor coaches and dining

The entrance to Monkton Combe station on 23 June 1952 as modified by the film company for 'The Titfield Thunderbolt'. (Author)

car representing the Cornish Riviera Express ran over the line, very probably the longest passenger train ever to do so. The event lasted quite a time in people's memories: during World War II evacuees sent to the area visited Camerton to see where the filming had taken place.

In November 1937 Dunkerton Colliery Sidings were used to film the night scenes of the Edgar Wallace thriller *Kate Plus Ten*. In 1952, following the complete closure of the line, it was used for filming Ealing Studio's delightful comedy *The Titfield Thunderbolt*. Most of the scenes were filmed in or around

The Liverpool & Manchester Railway *Lion* temporarily renamed *Thunderbolt* for the film. This 1952 view depicts it at Monkton Combe with 0-4-2T No 1401 hauling the ex-Kelvedon & Tollesbury Light Railway coach. (M E J Deane)

Monkton Combe station, temporarily renamed 'Titfield'. Used in the film was the Liverpool & Manchester Railway's 0-4-2 *Lion*, built in 1838 and believed to be the oldest working locomotive in the world. Temporarily renamed *Thunderbolt* for the film, she lacked power and could only manage a speed of about 15mph when running on the level without a load. To make her appear to run at a respectable speed when hauling a train an ex-GWR 0-4-2T acted as a banker and, braking sharply out of shot, allowed *Lion* to go on by herself. The maximum speed attained by this method was 30mph.

5 Broad Gauge Lines: The Bristol & Exeter Railway

THE BRISTOL & EXETER Railway was a relatively easy line to construct, its chief engineering features mainly deep cuttings at the Bristol end of the line. Its parliamentary bill received little opposition and the company had no problem in getting its shares taken. Construction work started in 1837 but problems arose later that year when an economic depression proved that some of the subscribers were men of straw, unable to pay the calls on their shares; in fact no less than 4000 out of a total of 15,000 shares were forfeited through this cause. It was decided that in order to conserve capital no outlay would be made on locomotives and rolling stock, so the line was leased to the GWR. It opened as far as Bridgwater on 14 June 1841.

Contracts for building the section to Taunton had been let in the spring of 1841 and the line extended to the town on 1 July 1842. On 5 January 1843 trains worked through to a temporary terminus at Beam Bridge, near the eastern portal of the incomplete 1088yd Whiteball Tunnel and eventually through to Exeter on 1 May 1847. The return journey of the special Exeter to London left at 5.20pm and arrived at Paddington at 10.00pm. Sir Thomas Acland, one of its passengers, immediately went to the House of Commons and at 10.30pm stood up and informed the House that he had been in Exeter at 5.20pm – a vast contrast to the stage coach travel of only a few years before.

Leaving Bristol, where the Bristol & Exeter Railway had its terminus set at right angles to that of the GWR, the line in Somerset passes Long Ashton Platform, opened on 12 July 1926 and closed on 6 January 1941. Beyond the 110yd Flax Bourton Tunnel was the first Flax Bourton station, opened in 1860 and closed on 2 March 1893 when it was replaced by another of the same name over ¼ mile further west. The waiting shelter of the new station, which closed on 2 December 1963, is now on the down platform at Crowcombe on the West Somerset Railway. To the west of Flax Bourton were Tyntesfield Sidings, laid by

From Puxton signal box is this view of the Ministry of Transport pulverised fly ash sidings in use 1970-1 for M5 motorway construction. No 6981 and No 6875 are backing the train into the siding, 20 April 1970. (Revd Alan Newman)

Nailsea & Backwell station of Brunellian design, built by the Bristol & Exeter Railway. This view was taken on 1 June 1966. Beyond the station building is a large rectangular nameboard and on a lamp post nearer the photographer, is a small lozenge-shaped sign. Beyond the stone building is a timber-built parcels office. Adjacent to the signal box is the signal lamp room. At the end of the platform the signalman has parked his Vespa motor scooter with the red reflector facing away from oncoming trains to avoid confusing engine drivers in hours of darkness. (Author)

the Ministry of Fuel & Power in 1956—7 and closed in May 1981. The Brunel-designed stone station building at Nailsea & Backwell has been destroyed and replaced by bus-stop type shelters. Much of the platform was of timber because the first station was built on an embankment and a relatively light construction was required to avoid subsidence.

Yatton was formerly an important junction with branches formerly to Clevedon, the Cheddar Valley and Wrington, but happily it is still open as an ordinary station. The down platform has a Tudor-style building with a flat, all-round awning, while that on the up platform has an Italianate hipped roof with Tudor details. At the west end of the up platform is a canopy which came from Dauntsey station in Wiltshire and at one time also spanned the Clevedon bay platform at Yatton.

Yatton used to be a very busy station. In October 1920 the staff comprised a station master, a goods clerk, two passenger clerks, an inspector, a foreman,

Porter Kath Fear at
Yatton c 1950.
(Author's collection)

Mixed gauge at
Yatton 20 May 1892
– the last day of the
broad gauge.
Railway servants
crossed over the
track from one
platform to another
– notice the step on
the far left – but
passengers were
requested to use the
bridge. There is a
GPO box in the wall
that is emptied three
times daily, weekdays
only. To the right of
the door is a box for
collecting used books
and magazines for a
charity, the name of
which cannot be
read. Advertisements
include those for the
Strand Magazine, the
Illustrated London
News, the Bristol
Times & Mirror and
the adjacent hotel
and posting house.
(Author's collection)

three ticket collectors, two parcel porters, seven
porters, three shunters, a checker, a goods porter,
two passenger guards (one a rail motor
conductor), a goods guard, two travelling
porters, a signal lampman, eight signalmen, two
assistant signalmen and two telegraphists.

By 1888 W.H. Smith & Sons had opened a
bookstall on the up platform and in the late
1920s the GWR employed a refreshment boy to
sell chocolate and cigarettes. He was paid 15s
weekly plus 6d in the £ commission on his sales. Wyman's opened a bookstall,
probably the one formerly used by W.H. Smith's, on the up platform about 1932
and as it sold confectionery the lad was made redundant. The stall was very
busy, employing a manager, an assistant manager and six boys full time on paper
rounds. Two more boys were employed to carry chocolate and tobacco trays.
Some deceitful passengers deliberately delayed asking for items on the trays until
just before a train's departure, thus avoiding payment. A boy had to foot the loss
from his 10s weekly wage. The bookstall closed around 1966, about the date the
Clevedon branch closed.

The goods yard handled a considerable volume of traffic. Apart from coal,
farm implements arrived as did basic slag and other fertilisers, animal feeding
stuffs, building supplies and general goods for shops, while Yatton gas works
received one or two wagons of coal weekly. On Mondays, market days, cattle
were despatched.

Train movements were controlled from Yatton West signal box, built to a
Bristol & Exeter design. Measuring 50ft by 14ft, it housed a 53-lever frame; the
building was extended to 75ft in 1897. In 1917 a new 129-lever frame was
fitted. The busy signal box was manned by two signalmen and a boy. It closed
on 31 January 1972 when colour light signalling was introduced.

About 1940 Yatton station played host to King George VI and Queen Elizabeth when the Royal Train was stabled at the station for two nights. Cows were removed from nearby fields so that the royal party would not be disturbed by their night-time lowing, and the Wells goods was cancelled in the interests of quiet. Sawdust was laid in order to deaden the footsteps of the bodyguards. Needless to say, no shunting was carried out on those nights, which meant that the goods train did not arrive at Clevedon until mid-morning. Guard Albert Maslin carried telegraph messages from Yatton booking office to the royal coach.

Puxton, closed on 6 April 1964, had a siding serving a milk depot. Worle Parkway opened on 24 September 1990 at a cost of £700,000. As it was built on marshy ground, materials used for construction were as light as possible. Intended only for local trains, the platforms are too short to hold an HST, though plans are being made for the platforms to be extended. A large car park is adjacent.

Beyond is Worle Junction where the Weston super Mare loop line goes off to the right. Before the opening of that loop Weston super Mare was served by a terminal branch line that left the main line at Weston Junction. The opening

An 'Achilles' class 4-2-2 with the down 'Flying Dutchman' passes the water tank at Old Weston Junction, 1894. (Author's collection)

The up broad gauge 'Cornishman' passing Worle signal box. Worle station on the Weston super Mare loop can be seen to the left of the signal box, 3 May 1892. (Author's collection)

At Uphill Junction the down broad gauge 'Cornishman' hauled by *Emperor* passes a standard gauge goods train on the Weston super Mare Loop *c* May 1892. (Author's collection)

The up 'Flying Dutchman' hauled by the broad gauge *Balaclava* near Uphill Junction, 19 May 1892. (Author's collection)

of the loop on 1 March 1884 rendered Weston Junction redundant so it closed on the same date. The Weston loop rejoins the main line at Uphill Junction. Uphill Cutting, 69ft deep, has an impressive Grade II flying arch with a span of 115½ft carrying the road 63ft above the railway.

An interesting project which, had it come to fruition, would have made far-reaching changes on the hinterland, was the Brean Down Harbour Company, incorporated in 1862. There were visions of it becoming a great transatlantic port, as the distance from London to Brean Down was only 140 miles compared with the 200 miles from London to Liverpool, thus shortening the railway journey by at least an hour. The prospectus said that 'Brean Down Harbour will also furnish an excellent landing place for cattle and other livestock from the South of Ireland'. Another point in its favour was that 'The proximity to the Welsh Coal Fields will afford ample facilities for a cheap and expeditious supply of the best steam coal for the steamers using the harbour'. On 5 November 1864 the PS *Wye* conveyed a party of dignitaries to lay the foundation stone of the new harbour. She had left Bristol the previous day but owing to the dense fog it was doubtful whether she would be able to reach Weston. She succeeded in doing so and Lady Wilmot, wife of the harbour company's chairman, was able to lay the stone.

The undertaking quickly ran into trouble – in fact on the first tide. The stone was marked by a buoy attached to a cable so short that it failed to allow for the unusually high tide rise of the Bristol Channel. The result was that the buoy floated away, carrying the stone with it. The following year the harbour company was empowered to construct a 3¼-mile rail link from Bleadon station. Because of financial difficulties the harbour works progressed slowly and on 9 December 1872 a violent storm almost completely destroyed the only jetty built and the project was abandoned.

Bleadon station closed on 5 October 1964. The timber-platformed Brean Road Halt opened on 17 June 1929 and closed on 2 May 1955. The station

The PS *Wye* following the laying of the foundation stone of the Brean Down breakwater. (Author's collection)

The timber buildings at Brent Knoll station, opened in 1875, 34 years after the line opened, and closed on 4 January 1971. The building material was selected because of the softness of the ground. Notice the attractive, typically Bristol & Exeter, bargeboards on the end of the nearest building. At the far end of the building is a 'Gentlemen' sign and attached to the end of this sign is the figure '3' denoting to a driver of a 3-car diesel multiple-unit where to stop. The view was taken on 1 June 1966. (Author)

buildings at Brent Knoll, closed to passengers on 4 January 1971, were constructed of timber and displayed attractive bargeboards – a distinctive feature of many Bristol & Exeter stations.

Highbridge was another former junction station, where the Somerset Central Railway from Glastonbury to Burnham on Sea crossed the Bristol & Exeter just north of the station. The original station building was destroyed in the 1970s and replaced with small shelters.

Dunball station opened in 1873 and closed on 5 October 1964. It had staggered platforms because it stood on either side of King's Sedgemoor Drain and wooden shelters stood on timber platforms. It was the junction of a short branch to Dunball Wharf.

Bridgwater, a Brunel Grade II listed station, has Georgian-style windows and a low pitched roof almost entirely concealed beneath parapets. The buildings on both platforms match. At one time British Cellophane Ltd had sidings north of the station. Initially, shunting was carried out by the firm's 0-4-0 saddle tank engines and latterly by British Railways diesel-mechanical 0-6-0 No D2133. North-west of the passenger station are facilities for handling waste containers from Hinkley Point Nuclear Power Station. An earlier dispatch from Bridgwater was elvers, Gloucester merchants demanding up to a ton per day.

Just south of the station were the Bristol & Exeter Railway's carriage and wagon works, once one of the town's major employers. During the 1930s the

Bridgwater, view up, 1897. The large corrugated-iron parcels and cloak room with a clerestory roof is of unusual design. Notice the windbreak across the platform beyond. (Author's collection)

Staff outside Bridgwater's Bristol & Exeter booking office, 1859. The man second from the left holds a shunting pole. (P J Squibbs collection)

0-6-0PT No 2127 in Bridgwater goods yard on 13 October 1951. The position of the headlamps seems to indicate that it is an express passenger train, whereas in reality it is the station pilot code of 1 white and 1 red lamp. The engine was withdrawn six months after this picture was taken. (Colin Roberts)

Coal wagons derailed on a crossover at Bridgwater *c* 1935. The Docks branch curves left. (Author's collection)

works changed over to tarpaulin sheet examination and during World War II its facilities were used for repairing all types of military canvas, such as tents and stretchers. Eventually returned to civilian use, the works caught fire early on 25 August 1947. Approximately 1500 sheets and hundreds of pulley blocks were destroyed and the works never re-opened. Every tarpaulin was numbered and each rope had a numbered ferrule. Every few years, at a given weekend, a census was taken of sheets, ropes and wagons on all railways in Britain and was submitted to the Railway Clearing House. Hennet & Co, wagon builders and general engineers, also trading in the town, was taken over by the Bridgwater Engineering Co Ltd which ceased trading in 1878—9.

The low-lying section of railway south of Bridgwater was subject to flooding – for instance on 20 November 1875 an extra engine was coupled to a train and, by running very slowly so as not to scoop too much water into the fireboxes, it could be safely drawn through the flood water, though by the time

dry land was reached steam was just about exhausted and the fires were out. It had taken approximately nine minutes to pass through floodwater 1½ mile long and 3ft deep. It was a similar story in the following year when water 5ft 3in deep covered the line for five weeks. On that occasion only the parapet rail of the bridge over the River Parrett was visible above the water.

Durston station opened on 1 October 1853, together with the branch to Yeovil, and closed on 5 October 1964. The down platform, of island pattern, served the down main line on one side and branch trains on the other. Originally a train shed covered the branch platform. The shortened route to the west from Paddington joined at Cogload Junction. It was a 'flying junction', a clever design so that the down line from Bristol was carried over the two lines via Castle Cary so that no train was delayed by a conflicting movement. In the early 1930s the track was quadrupled from Cogload Junction through Taunton to Norton Fitzwarren, an improvement particularly useful on busy summer Saturdays. That widening work was carried out under the Development (Loans Guarantees & Grants) Act of 1929 which, with the aim of reliev-ing national unemployment, provided funds for the improvement of large public works.

Creech St Michael Halt opened on 13 August 1928 at a cost of £600 and had to be extensively modified three years later when the track through the station was quadrupled. Only the outer tracks had platforms. Unlike most halts, it was staffed. It closed on 5 October 1964. Beyond, the line burrowed beneath the Chard Canal. Due to the dip, water collected under the aqueduct and

A 2-4-0 with water to footplate level passes through floods at Creech Junction with an up train *c* 1887. Notice the windmill, left. (Author's collection)

Durston Junction, view towards Weston super Mare, 21 August 1962. (Author)

Passenger station staff at Taunton, 1885. (Author's collection)

Taunton station being extended July 1895. Left can be seen the train shed and right is part of the locomotive shed. One small girl is among many males. (Author's collection)

needed to be pumped to surface drains. The Bristol & Exeter eventually purchased and closed the waterway but the invert was not filled and the line raised until 1895.

Creech Troughs, opened in 1902 to enable locomotives to pick up water at speed, unusually were filled with water from the Bridgwater & Taunton Canal that ran at a slightly higher level than the railway. As many as 54 locomotives took water daily from those troughs in 1904.

As Taunton station was situated on the northern edge of the town, initially it was of Brunel's one-sided pattern. The up and down platforms were both sited on the same side of the track, the advantage being that passengers did not have to cross a line to reach the required platform. That was all well and good in the early days when trains were relatively few and far between, but as it meant that an up train had to cross to the down line to reach the platform and then cross it again when leaving, the feature led to delays when trains became more frequent. In 1868 Taunton was given a conventional station with up and down

Semaphore signals form an interesting view from the front seat of a Taunton to Minehead diesel multiple-unit, 1 February 1969. (W H Harbor)

No 7326 at Taunton heading the 11.15am to Barnstaple Junction, 9 August 1963. D1039 *Western King* heads an express to Exeter. (Author)

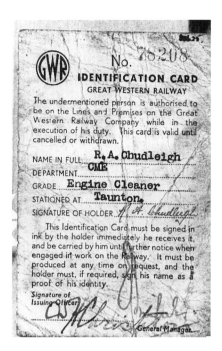

A GWR identity card. 'CME' is 'Chief Mechanical Engineer'. (Author)

platforms on different sides. At that date it was also given a train shed but lost it when the line was quadrupled.

The maximum number of staff employed by the GWR at Taunton in all departments peaked at around 1800 in 1943. North of the station was the GWR concrete depot. Opened in 1898 to produce such items as fence and loading gauge posts, paving stones and signal box coal bins, in more recent years it turned out sleepers and bridge sections.

A large, new brick-built goods depot opened on 20 February 1932. At the loading dock a 6-ton manual crane dealt with container traffic and other heavy consignments, while the whole length of the shed was served by overhead gantry cranes consisting of manual block and tackle with 1-ton capacity. Two electrically-powered lifts gave access to the overhead warehouse used mainly for storing animal feedstuffs. Each firm using the warehouse was charged for the space it occupied.

Inwards traffic, in addition to a heavy tonnage of coke and coal, was frozen meat from Avonmouth and London docks, biscuits, building materials, farm supplies and hides for local tanneries. Outwards traffic tended to be connected with agriculture. Taunton handled an exceptional volume of livestock and a new cattle dock was opened at the east end of the goods depot, conveniently near the cattle market. Fresh meat was collected from local abattoirs and sent from Taunton to Smithfield Market. From October to March a huge quantity of sugar beet was sent to a sugar factory at Kidderminster and also to Kingswinford, near Wolverhampton, for jam making. A GWR Fordson tractor and trailer called at each farm and railway staff tossed the beet into the trailer using special pronged forks with bulbous ends to protect the beet from damage. The forks alone were heavy and considerable strength and effort were required to throw a load over the timber sides. As the tractor driver and his mate had no protection from the weather, it was a particularly unpleasant job in wet weather. On arrival at Taunton the beet had to be transhipped into railway wagons. Butter, eggs, potatoes, greenstuffs and pit props were the principal items sent away by rail.

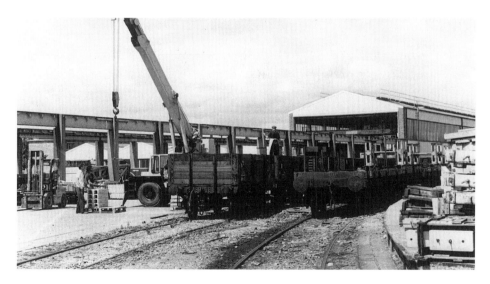

The concrete depot at Taunton, 1 August 1979. (Author)

Until the early 1950s the delivery of consignments to shops and merchants in Taunton was by horse and dray, typical loads being cigarettes in cardboard boxes, casks of china, rolls of lead, barrels of vinegar, goods in crates and cardboard cases. Weighty articles were off-loaded using cartage skids – two lengths of wood about 12ft in length with a hook at one end to catch on the side of the dray, the other end resting on the ground. Goods were then slid down the two strips, chains keeping the lengths from spreading too far apart.

Although railwaymen were generally honest, at one period habitual pilfering was experienced from consignments of tobacco carried on one of the branch line trucks. The Railway Police were alerted and the local detective based at Taunton decided to conceal himself in a large laundry basket that had been specially provided. He carefully observed the operations at stations along the branch and eventually discovered the culprit, but *en route* was deliberately given a few rough shunts by the train crew who knew of his mission.

In 1963 all local goods yards were closed and all freight for the area centred on Taunton, which became a Freight Concentration Depot. However, the development of motorways and supermarkets with their own road transport led to such a reduction in traffic by rail that the depot closed in 1972.

Beyond the goods loop that allowed freight trains to avoid the passenger platforms was Taunton West Yard and the 7-road Fairwater Yard, built early in World War II and from 1960 used by the chief Civil Engineer for assembling and loading track. In 2006 it became a Freightliner Heavy Haul High Output Operations Base. To the west was Silk Mills level crossing, replaced by a bridge in 2005. Beyond, a siding to a sugar beet factory was opened on 29 August 1929 and 13 years later became Blinkhorn Sidings, serving a United States' Army store. The site of that is now a trading estate.

The original two-road Norton Fitzwarren station opened on 1 June 1873 and was rebuilt when the line was quadrupled. Its goods yard dealt with large quantities of cider apples. The station closed on 30 October 1961. About one mile to the west was Victory Siding, chiefly used for loading sugar beet; and a

Norton Fitzwarren *c* 1903. The Barnstaple and Minehead lines branch off right beyond the platform. A hand crane can be seen in the goods yard, right. The wide distance between the up and down tracks indicates that it was formerly a broad gauge line. (Author's collection)

An up broad gauge express at Norton Fitzwarren *c* 1891. Branches to Barnstaple and Minehead curve right. Notice the mixed gauge track. (Author's collection)

further 3 miles beyond was Poole Siding, serving a brick and tile works.

Wellington was originally a two-road station but in 1932–3 the platforms were moved outwards to be served by loops, through trains being allowed to overtake using the new centre roads. The station closed on 5 October 1964. Beyond the station, Wellington Bank rises at a gradient of 1 in 80/90 for 3¾ miles. On weekdays in 1939 three banking engines were on duty on turns of about eight hours each to assist freight trains up the gradient. It had been the scene of the exploit of the *City of Truro* on 9 May 1904 when it reached 102.3mph descending the bank. The line enters the Whiteball Tunnel of 1088yd and emerges in the county of Devon.

One Wellington porter obtained more than his fair share of tips from first-class passengers. Eventually his colleagues decided they could stand no more and must teach him a lesson. One day when he had carried luggage into a compartment and was placing it on the rack after the carriage door had been closed the guard waved the train off with the porter still aboard. His colleagues called out to him not to worry as they would get the signalman at the next box to stop the train and let him out. They kept their word and from Whiteball the porter cadged a lift on the footplate of a returning banking engine. The driver, also in the joke, opened the regulator wide. The engine roared through the tunnel at about 70mph, rocking and swaying and thoroughly frightening the porter. And still they had not finished with him. The driver feigned a heart attack and collapsed. The porter, amazed that the fireman did not take over the controls, yelled 'Can't you stop it?' 'No', he replied, 'I don't know how, I only came on the job last week!' The terrified porter, white with fear, climbed down the cab steps and was prepared to leap off the rapidly-moving engine. Only then was it revealed as a joke. The lesson had certainly been learned and he never purposely sought large tips again.

The Portishead Branch

The first suggestion for a line to Portishead was made as early as 1800. A Mr Grace of Portishead proposed building a line to link the local collieries with his wharf at Portishead tide mill. The railway was cunningly planned to be built on a gradient so that descending loaded wagons could draw up the empties, but the scheme proved abortive. The next plan was also unorthodox. In order to avoid the difficulties of navigating the twisting River Avon to Bristol, schemes were afoot for building docks at Portbury. In May 1845 Brunel planned to connect the village with Bristol by means of an atmospheric railway.

With that system, like the contemporary one he was installing on the South Devon Railway, locomotives were dispensed with and a leading truck was

equipped with a piston that fitted into a pipe set between the rails. Pumping stations built every few miles apart extracted air in front of the piston so that air pressure would push along the piston and also the train. The Portbury Pier & Railway Company obtained its Act in 1846 but was wound up in 1851 through lack of funds. That was just as well as the atmospherically-worked South Devon Railway proved a failure because the leather seal on top of the pipe could not hold the vacuum. Locomotive haulage had to be introduced instead.

Finally, in 1863 the Bristol & Portbury Pier & Railway Company obtained an Act to build a broad gauge line from a junction with the Bristol & Exeter Railway at Bedminster to a pier at Portbury with a subsidiary branch running to Portishead. In the event a change of plan caused the company to abandon the Portbury terminus and make the Portishead branch the main line. The Act stated that the amenities of the Ham Green Estate were to be preserved by carrying the railway through two tunnels, but during construction work that plan was modified by replacing the tunnel to the east of the site of the later Ham Green Halt with a cutting.

The 9½-mile line opened on 18 April 1867. It was worked by the Bristol & Exeter Railway, the GWR purchasing the line on 1 July 1884. In 1871 a bill had been promoted to make Portishead Pill into a dock. The Avonmouth Company, on the opposite bank of the Avon, also had plans that year, so both were competing for a subscription of £100,000 from Bristol Corporation. The first ship to enter Portishead Dock was the railway company's paddle steamer *Lyn* on 28 June 1879. The Portishead Railway had been enterprising enough to operate steamer services across the Bristol Channel to Newport and Cardiff all the year round, with special excursions to Ilfracombe in the summer and through rail and steamer bookings from both the GWR and the Midland Railway. The

Constructing the Portishead line near the site of Clifton Bridge station, *c* 1866. (Author's collection)

ferry to South Wales certainly filled a need as the Severn Tunnel was not opened to passenger traffic until 1 December 1886. The GWR then abandoned the ferry on 1 October 1886. It is interesting to record that until about July 1875 all goods traffic on the Portishead line was carried by passenger train. The line was converted to standard gauge between 24 and 27 January 1880.

The branch was used for an interesting experiment. In the early days of railways, in the event of an emergency, passengers had no means of communication with a driver apart from using their voices. In 1864 Portishead trains were equipped with a cord run from the front brake van of a passenger train to a large warning gong on the side of the locomotive's tender. By 1869 that system had been modified and improved so that the cord extended through rings along the eaves of all coach roofs and was linked to the emergency whistle on the engine, rather than a gong on the tender. That allowed anyone on the train, so long as they were able to lean out of the window and tug the cord, to warn the driver.

On 23 June 1874 a Bristolian, Reuben Lyon, used the branch to test a further development. That consisted of a bellows and handle fixed to each compartment of a set of three coaches. By pulling down a handle air was blown from the bellows through a pipe to both the guard's van and the engine where it sounded whistles inserted into the ends of the pipes. In addition, the handle raised an arm (or a light at night) to indicate the compartment in which the apparatus had been used. That arm was cunningly placed so that it could not be lowered while the train was moving. The pipes doubled as a speaking tube between the front and rear guards or between a guard and the driver. The inventor tried it with 300ft of tube, equivalent to ten or twelve coaches, and the six whistles invariably worked. The system was not adopted as it was more expensive to install and maintain than a simple cord and did not have any great advantages. In the following year communication by electric bell was tried but with no permanent success.

Portishead power station was enlarged after World War II and to carry out the project the Central Electricity Authority took over the site of Portishead railway station and provided a replacement. Then on 7 September 1964 passenger services on the branch were withdrawn, even though as recently as Whit Monday 1963 400 passengers had travelled to Portishead on the 11.40am from Temple Meads. Regular freight trains continued until 30 March 1981. British Railways retained the line out of use in the hope that traffic from the new Portbury Docks would increase and also that the line might be involved in a Bristol Metro scheme.

The line lay derelict until 2001 when the track was re-laid from Parson Street Junction, Bristol, to Pill. Pill Viaduct was repaired by drilling out flaking bricks, replacing them and generally re-pointing. From Pill a new 1.2-mile section was built to serve Portbury Docks. A lake had to be filled in to make an embankment and the lake re-created elsewhere as it was of special environmental interest. The cost of all work on the branch totalled £21 million. It re-opened officially to traffic on 21 December 2001 when 0-6-0ST *Portbury*, formerly belonging to the Port of Bristol Authority, hauled a three-coach passenger train to Portbury Docks. Regular freight traffic started on 7 January 2002 and the line currently carries coal trains and about 500,000 imported cars annually.

The first Somerset station on the branch was the delightfully named Nightingale Valley Halt, opened on 9 July 1928. Set beside the Avon almost below Clifton Suspension Bridge, it was intended for use by day-trippers in the summer months. It was cheaply constructed from old railway sleepers surmounted by a corrugated-iron shelter for times of sun or rain. The halt was little used and at the end of the summer of 1932 closed on 12 September never to re-open.

Beyond, the line enters the 232yd Clifton Bridge No 2 Tunnel and the 88-yd Sandstone Tunnel before arriving at a passing loop at Oakwood signal box, opened on 14 May 1929 to break up the 4½ miles of single line between Clifton Bridge and Pill. Ham Green Halt, opened on 23 December 1926, served a nearby hospital and village. Unusually it was given two pagoda shelters, indicative of the traffic it enjoyed. In 1939 electric lighting was installed at a cost of £105. During World War II part of Ham Green Hospital was used by United States forces and they brought more traffic to the halt. The 665yd Pill Tunnel is beyond and the line crossed the viaduct to the double-tracked Pill station. The main building was at road level and brick-built shelters on the platforms.

The ex-Port of Bristol Authority No 34 *Portbury* approaching Pill Viaduct with the re-opening train, 21 December 2001. It displays the Railtrack headlight. (Author)

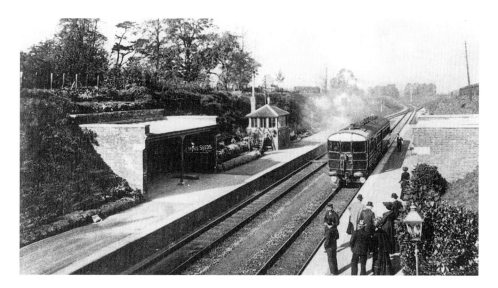

West of the station site a new section of line serves Portbury Docks, but the original line curved round to Portbury Shipyard station, opened on 16 September 1918 to serve a new shipyard begun to replace vessels lost by enemy action. With the armistice on 11 November 1918 the project was abandoned but the site was used by Admiralty personnel, so the timber platform and shelter were kept open until 26 March 1923.

Portbury station had an impressive station building incorporating offices and a station master's house. Portishead originally had a single platform with an

Steam railmotor No 58 at Pill *c* 1910. In the waiting shelter is an enamel sign advertising Sutton's seeds. During World War I the GWR negotiated with this firm to supply railwaymen with seeds at a favourable rate in order to encourage staff to work an allotment to help ease the wartime food shortage. (Author's collection)

Portbury Shipyard station, only open from 16 September 1918 to 26 March 1923. (M J Tozer collection)

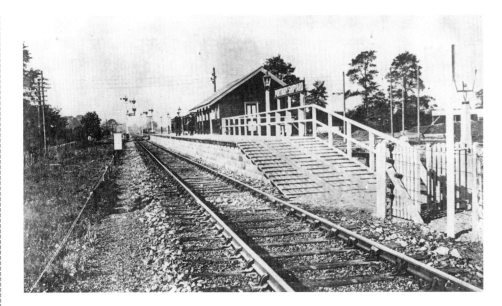

The domestic style of architecture is evident at Portbury station, 5 September 1958. It is unusual in not being adorned with posters, advertisements or timetables. The corrugated-iron lamp hut is nearest the photographer. (Author)

The original Portishead station, 9 April 1953. (Dr A J G Dickens)

even grander building than Portbury and in 1929 a timber and cinder platform was built on the up side of the line. The brick-built engine shed closed in 1896. In 1954 a new station was built of pre-stressed concrete and local stone. Built on a marsh, problems of subsidence were experienced until its closure in 1964. It now forms part of the Station Garage. The docks were shunted by Port of Bristol Authority locomotives. In the 1960s Albright & Wilson, manufacturers of phosphorous, distributed their product from Portishead in specially-built rail tank wagons holding a pay load of 22¼ tons each. As phosphorous was susceptible to spontaneous combustion in contact with air, it was loaded and discharged in water at a temperature of 60 degrees Centigrade. Full tank wagons travelled with a water 'blanket' and the tanks were filled with water for their return journey, both on safety grounds and to protect the tank shell from internal attack by acids formed from residues in the tanks. Between 36 and 40 tankers a week were handled. Other traffic on the branch included timber, grain and paper, while local power stations used coal and oil. In 1971 a wood pulp terminal opened at Portishead Dock and pulp was loaded direct into bulk trains to convey it to Marsh Ponds, east of Temple Meads, conveniently near the paper mill. That traffic had ceased by 1980.

Albright & Wilson Ltd's Peckett 0-4-0ST built in 1923 at Bristol. The photograph was taken on 22 May 1964. (Revd Alan Newman)

The Yatton to Clevedon Branch

The 3½-mile Bristol & Exeter Railway branch from Yatton to Clevedon was constructed quite cheaply over the flat moors. It carried no fewer than 2000 passengers on the opening day 28 July 1847. The volume of traffic to the watering place increased to such an extent that a special 560ft excursion platform was built and remained until 1879. The branch was converted from broad to standard gauge on a single day, Sunday 28 September 1879. About 160 men were split into gangs and started work at midnight on Saturday. By 4pm on the Sunday afternoon the track had been narrowed and tested by a

No 1463, having arrived at Yatton with the 10.30am mixed train from Clevedon, shunts off the goods wagons and brake van from behind the two auto coaches. A porter is whitewashing the platform edge, 13 June 1957. (Author)

No 41207 arrives at Yatton on 12 June 1963 with the last train of empty wagons, Clevedon goods depot having closed on 8 June 1963. (M Wathen)

locomotive and coach running over the line. The normal service was resumed on Monday.

The branch saw some interesting locomotive power. Soon after its opening it was used for the trials of a combined engine and carriage constructed at Fairfield Works, Bow, in 1848 and named *Fairfield*. Painted

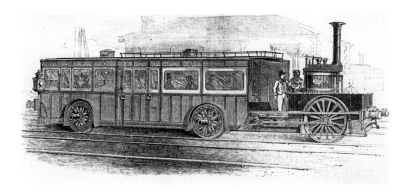

sky blue, it was 40ft long and had six wheels. The two driving wheels were of metal but the remaining ones of timber. The boiler was set vertically and consumed 14.8 lb of coal per mile. It was the first workable self-propelled railcar to run a regular passenger service and the multiple unit diesel of today can trace its ancestry back to that machine.

Sixty years later steam railcars again replaced a separate locomotive and coaches. Two cars were stabled at Yatton, one travelling as far as Swindon each day. In 1917 as a wartime economy measure those railmotors were worked without a guard, the first section of the GWR to experience such an economy. In 1925 an average of four coal and mineral wagons were received daily in addition to seven goods wagons received and three despatched. Fifty-three cattle trucks ran over the line that year and 2000 milk churns were carried. Between 1924 and 1936 Clevedon commuters enjoyed a through carriage to and from Bristol. In the evening it was slipped from the main line train at Yatton and worked in by the branch train. In the 1930s some of the early GWR diesel railcars used the branch at a time when such trains were a rare sight indeed. It was finally dieselised in 1960.

In the days of steam one of the interesting features of the branch was auto train working. The tank engine pulled the coaches to Clevedon and then, to avoid wasting time uncoupling and running the engine round its train, the locomotive remained at what was now the rear of the train and pushed it to Yatton, the driver walking to a special driving compartment at the end of the coach which now became the front. Although an engine that was not equipped for auto working should have run round its train at the end of each journey, in practice a blind eye was often turned to that regulation. Although on the return trip from Clevedon to Yatton the driver stood in the control vestibule of the auto coach, it was just show; his fireman on the engine was actually both driving and firing.

A train should show a white light at the front and a red light at the rear. On arrival at Clevedon or Yatton it was the driver's responsibility to take the red shade out of the trailing end lamp and the fireman's job to put the red shade in at the engine end. Although a red shade was supposed to be put in at the trailing end, a regular signalman at Yatton turned a blind eye if the rule was not observed because safety was not compromised in any way.

One day there was a relief signalman at Yatton and when the guard gave the driver the 'Right away', the signal was not pulled off. A porter went across to

The Bristol & Exeter Railway's combined steam engine and coach, No 29 *Fairfield*. Built in 1848 it worked on the Yatton to Clevedon branch *c* 1849. As the floor was within 9in of the rails it required no platform. The forward saloon accommodated 16 first-class passengers and that at the rear 32 in the second class. Luggage was carried on the roof as was contemporary custom. (Author's collection)

the signal box to enquire why and, informed that the train was showing a red light at the front, reported that to the fireman who lifted the red shade and the signal came off. Seeing that, the fireman dropped the red shade and the signal went on. He lifted the shade and the signal was pulled off; he dropped the shade again and the signal was returned again. The procedure continued for a while but eventually the signal went on and stayed that way even though the shade was lifted.

The fireman went to the box and requested that the signal be pulled off. The signalman replied that the train was not going to leave until a white light was showing at the front as stated in the regulations. For the rest of the evening the correct procedure was carried out.

The next day the booking boy from the signal box went over to the engine shed and fetched a scuttle of coal as was the daily custom when the official supply to the signal box ran out. It was a large box and hard to heat and the regular supply was insufficient to feed the fires at each end of the box. Following the visit the shedman rang the box and asked the signalman to send the boy back with the coal that had been taken without authority. This he did. Footplate crews never experienced further trouble with signalmen.

During World War II tarpaulin sheets were fitted to locomotives at night to prevent enemy planes from seeing the fires. That made conditions on the footplate very hot and unpleasant, so as far as possible firemen on the branch tried to make up the fire under the roof at Clevedon so that the sheet could be left off. At other times on the branch it could be cold and draughty on the footplate when crossing the flat moors, so sheets were tied at the doorways.

The branch closed to goods traffic on 10 June 1963; Clevedon became an unstaffed halt on 20 April 1964 and services were withdrawn on 3 October 1966. The track was left *in situ* and the branch was used for storing vehicles such as the Newton Abbot to Edinburgh car sleeper on 9 July 1969. As 'Clevedon Siding', from 29 September 1969 to 5 February 1970 it was used for training Plassermatic crews in the art of using permanent way machines.

Curving away from the main line at Yatton, the Clevedon branch passed the locomotive shed and Wake & Dean's furniture siding on the right and Capern's bird seed siding on the left.

No 1463 pushes the two auto coaches out of Clevedon to Yatton, 25 April 1957. (Revd Alan Newman)

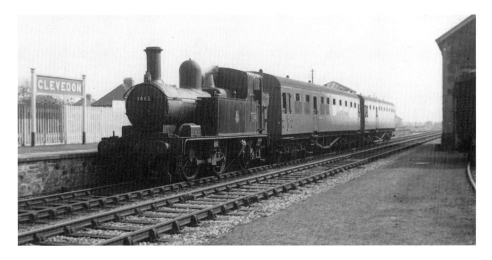

The interior of the train shed at Clevedon, 8 April 1964. (M Wathen)

The result of an engine thrusting two coaches through a wall into the street outside Clevedon station. Part of the locomotive can be seen on the left, its chimney dislodged. Most onlookers are male. This incident occurred *c* 1884. (Author's collection)

The original station offices and train shed at Clevedon were of timber but in 1890 the offices were rebuilt in local stone, harmonising well with its surroundings. Periodically, due to braking problems, a train would hit the buffers at Clevedon or Yatton, and on one occasion at Clevedon pushed the coaches into the road outside. The station was well used because apart from commuters to Bristol or Weston super Mare there were shoppers, tourists, schoolchildren travelling daily to Bristol, or from Yatton to Clevedon, and St

Brandon's School pupils with trunks at the beginning and end of term. In 1951 69,000 tickets were sold.

Apart from coal, inwards traffic consisted of goods for local shops, fertilisers, cattle feed, potatoes, timber for a local merchant, and a wagon of beer each week. Outwards traffic was containers of Hales' cakes, the firm receiving inwards ingredients of flour, sugar, margarine and dried fruit. Until the 1930s between 1 and 20 cases of boots were despatched daily. The Royal Naval Medical Research Centre at Clevedon carried out the development of penicillin and received containers of supplies.

In 1959 staff at Clevedon consisted of the station master, 2 booking clerks, 2 parcel porters, 2 platform porters, 1 female goods clerk from Yatton for part of the day, 1 goods porter, 1 checker and 2 lorry drivers

The engine shed at Clevedon closed in May 1879 when the locomotive was transferred to Yatton where a shed opened in that year; that remained in use until August 1960.

The Cheddar Valley Railway

The Cheddar Valley & Yatton Act of 1864 authorised the construction of a broad gauge single line from Yatton to a junction with the Somerset & Dorset Railway at Wells. The section from Yatton to Cheddar was opened on 3 August 1869 and the remainder on 5 April 1870. All the buildings were constructed in Mendip conglomerate in the usual Bristol & Exeter style and were a truly delightful set of *cottage orné* stations. The track was cross-sleepered and that eased its conversion to standard gauge between 15 and 18 November 1875, the line being unique in that it was the only section of the Bristol & Exeter to be converted during that company's existence. The line was closed to passengers from 9 September 1963. Cheddar to Congresbury closed completely on 1 October 1964 and to Yatton on 16 November 1964 and between Cheddar and Wells 29 April 1969.

Congresbury station was a typical, solid-looking standard Bristol & Exeter building with intricate bargeboards, decorative roof tiles and cruciform ridge tiles. An up platform was brought into use on 14 April 1901 in preparation for the opening of the Wrington Vale Light Railway. No bay platform was provided as light railway trains terminated at Yatton, not Congresbury. The building at Sandford & Banwell station was almost identical to that at Congresbury but only ever had a single platform. South of the station a line led to quarries of Roads Reconstruction Ltd which were worked by the firm's own locomotives.

The original Winscombe station was of timber construction and according to a contemporary edition

Poster advertising the cutting of the first sod of the Yatton & Cheddar Railway, 26 February 1867. (Author's collection)

YATTON & CHEDDAR VALLEY
RAILWAY.

THE FIRST SOD

OF THIS RAILWAY, WILL BE CUT

On Tuesday, the 26th Feb.

At 3 o'clock, on SHUTSHELVE HILL,

BY MRS. YATMAN,

OF WINSCOMBE HILL.

And a Procession

OF THE

Mayor & Corporation

Will be Formed at the TOWN HALL, Axbridge,

At 2 o'clock, where all Parties desirous of participating in the Ceremony, are requested to assemble.

AN EFFICIENT BAND WILL BE IN ATTENDANCE.

THERE WILL ALSO BE A

BALL IN THE EVENING,

At the Town-hall, at Half-past 8 o'clock,

Under the Patronage of the Mayor and Corporation.

Tickets may be had either of Mr. BROOKS, Mr. MAINE, or Mr. OLIVER, at 2s. 6d. each, to include Tea, Coffee, &c.

OLIVER & SON, Printers and Booksellers, AXBRIDGE.

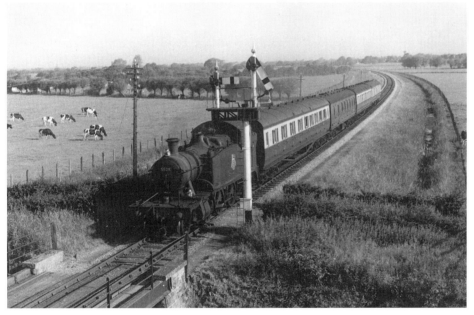

No 9668 at Congresbury with a Wells to Yatton train *c* 1961. (Author's collection)

No 5528 approaches Congresbury with the 7.58am Yatton to Witham, 17 June 1957. (Author)

of the *Bath Chronicle* looked like a 'Swiss chalet'. It was a timber replica of the stone station at Draycott, because the weight of a stone station on the newly-made embankment would have caused it to settle. In 1905 Winscombe was given a standard GWR red brick building, the original structure hauled by a traction engine to become part of a local shop. Until 1869 that station was called Woodborough but in that year was re-named to prevent confusion with the station of the same name in Wiltshire. The new name board was sent down from Bristol and the local carpenter spent a laborious afternoon and evening fixing it. For years the old man had successfully concealed the fact that he was illiterate, but the secret was out the next morning when passengers for the first train stared in amazement at the inverted board. Beyond the station the line passed through a spur on the Mendips in the 180yd Shute Shelve Tunnel, unlined except at the Yatton end. In 1947 GWR diesel railcar No 37 was destroyed by fire in that tunnel.

The twin platform Axbridge station was unusually set above the village whereas most stations, if not level with the settlement, were below. Strawberry traffic was most important. Although strawberries were grown at Axbridge in 1870 the variety did not travel well and it was not until Royal Sovereign was introduced about 1900 that the belt of rich red loam some 3 miles long and ¼ mile wide was used for the plants, and consignments of fruit were sent by special strawberry train for sale in South Wales, Birmingham, Manchester, Edinburgh and Glasgow. Land was so precious that between Axbridge and Lodge Hill even the soil between the railway track and the boundary fence was cultivated. The A371 Axbridge by-pass now runs along the railway formation and passes the still-extant buildings.

Loading strawberries at Cheddar c 1905. Passenger coaches stand at the rear of the train. The train shed can be seen on the left and also the Bristol & Exeter signal box. In the lower right hand corner are permanent way materials. (M J Tozer collection)

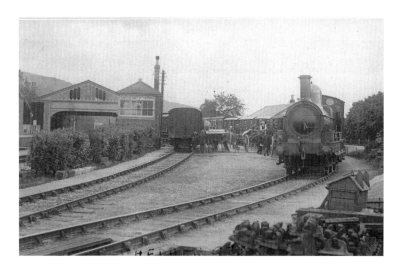

Cheddar station, expected to deal with considerable tourist traffic, was provided with a wooden train shed. Until 1925 it also boasted a refreshment room. The small, stone-built Draycott station was most attractive. Flanking it was a small signal box and wooden goods shed. Lodge Hill served the village of Westbury-sub-Mendip but was so named to avoid confusion with West-bury, Wiltshire.

Wookey station opened on 1 August 1871, just over a year after the other stations. The station building was of timber and was dominated by the large stone goods shed on the opposite side of the track. Apart from general traffic, the station dealt with trainloads of esparto grass from Avonmouth that arrived for St Cuthbert's Paper Mill. Paper was sent in return. Wells (Tucker Street) was the third station to be opened in the city and was the terminus of the line until through trains to Witham began on 1 January 1878. Unlike most Cheddar Valley stations it had two platforms.

At one time the branch dealt with a con-siderable volume of milk traffic, one train convey-

A 0-6-0 marooned at Draycott for three days in January 1963. The original of this postcard was well-worn. (Author's collection)

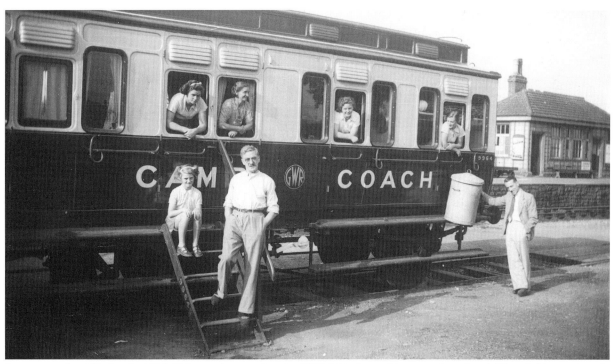

A camp coach at Wookey in 1934. This was the year that the GWR 'shirt button' logo was introduced. The ash bin was issued by the GWR. (M Flaherty)

A goods train from Bristol enters Wells, Tucker Street, behind No 46517 on 22 August 1957. This twin-pavilion Bristol & Exeter station was similar to those built by the Midland Railway. (Author)

Cheddar Valley
Buildings, Tucker
Street, Wells, built
by the Bristol &
Exeter Railway for
its staff. Notice the
barge boarding.
(Author)

ing eight vans for London. Before World War II that traffic died out because the Milk Marketing Board organised road collections.

The Wrington Vale Light Railway

The Wrington Vale Light Railway was authorised by a Light Railway Order in 1898 to build a branch from the Cheddar Valley line at Congresbury to Blagdon. Its estimated cost was £29,000 but unusually proved to be only £25,000. Obtaining a Light Railway Order rather than an Act of Parliament was far cheaper and also permitted a line to be more economically constructed by easing normal standards and permitting such things as ungated level crossings and a simpler signalling system. The line's expenses were less than £4000 a mile, whereas the Cheddar Valley line cost £12,000 per mile and the London Bridge-Charing Cross line no less than £1000 per yard.

No 41208
approaches Iwood
Lane ungated level
crossing *en route*
from Congresbury to
Wrington, 22
October 1962.
(Author)

The Wrington Vale line opened on 4 December 1901. All the stations were of brick and timber construction except Burrington, which at first had just a shelter, later replaced by stone buildings. Only two of the six level crossings had gates, the remainder being protected by cattle grids. The rails, instead of being held in chairs, were spiked directly to the sleepers and there were no signals apart from fixed distants. One development to boost traffic over the line was an excursion from Bristol to Langford by rail, onwards by George Young's charabanc through Burrington Combe to Cheddar and then return by rail. The trip also operated in the reverse direction. Bristol Tramways & Carriage Company buses started services in the area in 1921 and being more direct siphoned off much of the passenger traffic. The services were withdrawn on 14 September 1931, one of the first GWR branches to suffer.

The line proved invaluable for bringing machinery and materials to the Yeo Reservoir constructed at Blagdon and when the work was completed brought coal for the pumping station, a siding actually running into the building. Most of the land adjacent to the line was used for dairy farming and the branch proved useful for transporting milk, butter and cheese to markets in the days before

The last passenger train from Blagdon, 12 September 1931. Notice that the platform is low compared with the coach footboards. In the crowd are Driver Arthur Jones, Fireman Frank Salter and Guard Bert Maslen. This is another photo that has been well-used. (Author's collection)

A camp coach at Blagdon *c* 1936 after the branch had been closed to passenger traffic. The boy holds a container used for collecting water from the station buildings. (Author's collection)

rapid road travel. Sacks became a very important commodity on the branch during World War II. They were vital to the war effort, for besides being needed for sandbags to protect people and building from blast damage they were need for carrying grain and potatoes. They were stored in the redundant Blagdon station waiting room, ticket office and other buildings and also at Langford. Until 1940 the line carried about 2000 tons of coal annually to the Bristol Water Works Pumping Station at Blagdon. Interestingly, some of the coal came from Pensford & Bromley Colliery, a distance of 27½ miles by rail compared with 10 miles by road. Following the loss of that particular coal traffic, the remainder, chiefly coal, livestock and fertilisers to Langford, Burrington and Blagdon had become so light that those stations were closed completely on 1 November 1950.

Blagdon station looking very neglected on 27 August 1954. (Author)

Blagdon station in May 1963 after having been turned into a residence. An ex-GWR brake van is grounded nearby. (Author's collection)

The last coal arrived at Wrington on Friday 7 June 1963 and on the following day, although trains did not normally run on Saturdays, detonators exploded as the empties left the yard. The branch officially closed on 10 June 1963 and on that very day British Railways erected a new sign at Iwood ungated level crossing with the words 'Beware of Trains'. Following the line's closure the yard at Wrington continued in use as a coal depot, the fuel arriving by road.

The first engine to work the Wrington Vale Light Railway was a particularly interesting machine. It was 2-4-0T GWR No 1384 that had been built in 1875 for the Watlington & Princes Risborough Railway. When the GWR had finished with her she was sold to the Weston, Clevedon & Portishead Light Railway and named *Hesperus*. She ended her career rather ignominiously when a timber bridge at Wick St Lawrence collapsed under her weight.

The Weston super Mare Branch

At first Weston super Mare was served by a single broad gauge branch, 1½ mile long, that left the main line at Weston Junction on Hutton Moor approximately midway between the later Worle and Uphill Junctions. The branch opened on 14 June 1841 and trains were drawn by horses. Passenger trains generally consisted of three 4-wheeled unroofed coaches with hard, toast-rack seats pulled by three horses in tandem ridden by boys. Various accidents happened to both animals and their riders. In 1847 as the last train was proceeding along the branch line from Weston to the junction of the Great Western Railway to meet the two o'clock down train and the half past five up train, at a quarter of a mile from the station, one of the horses, suffering from a diseased heart, fell upon the rails and the carriages passed over it causing immediate death. The train was thrown off the line and the passengers finished the journey on foot. When the horses had to pull against the wind the 1½-mile journey took half an hour and many passengers preferred to walk down the line as it was quicker.

The first terminus at Weston super Mare and a train of three coaches hauled by three horses leaving for the main line at Weston Junction, 1846. (Author's collection)

Weston super Mare goods shed following an air raid on 28 and 29 June 1942. To the right can be seen part of Weston super Mare's second terminal station opened 20 July 1866, closed 1 March 1884 and converted to another goods shed in 1900-1. The scoop by the wagon was cunningly designed so that when filled with coal it could be easily slipped into the neck of a sack. (Author's collection)

As a consequence of a memorial presented to the railway company in October 1847, a steam-hauled express was worked from Weston super Mare to Bristol in the morning from the beginning of 1848, with a corresponding down train in the evening. Except for those two trains, the rest were worked by horses, and so for 3¼ years steam and animal traction were in use at the same time. Horses for the branch were provided by the GWR until the expiration of that company's lease on 30 April 1849 when the Bristol & Exeter worked its own system. From 1 April 1851 all trains to Weston were worked by locomotives.

The branch line followed the route of the present Winterstoke Road on the level to a single-story Gothic-style terminus designed by Brunel. It had but one platform and was set at the west end of Alexandra Parade. By the early 1860s traffic had developed to such an extent that the station proved inadequate, so the Bristol & Exeter's engineer, Francis Fox, designed a two-road station with a train shed. It was built south of the Locking Road of stone at a cost of £10,000. It opened on 20 July 1866 and the branch line was doubled on the same date. The station included a separate excursion platform.

To ease working a standard gauge Weston super Mare loop was opened on 1 March 1884. The terminal station, no longer required for passenger traffic, was relegated to the goods department. The excursion platform was retained and on 28 March 1907 was doubled in length and a bay line added. On 8 April

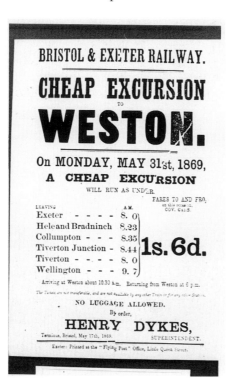

Bristol & Exeter Railway poster advertising a cheap excursion from Exeter to Weston super Mare on Whit Bank Holiday 31 May 1869. (Author's collection)

1914 the excursion station was further developed to give four, instead of two, platform faces. Independent of the main through station, it had its own ticket office and waiting room. On busy Bank Holidays up to 30,000 trippers arrived in thirty special trains. Weston was very popular for Sunday-school excursions: about 4000 children were there on 29 June 1909 and a total of 76,000 in June and July 1912. Rather surprisingly, the excursion platform was the starting point and terminus of the prestigious 'Bristolian' on summer Saturdays in 1952. The increased use of road transport led to the closure of the excursion station on 6 September 1964.

Two stations are provided on the Weston super Mare loop line. Weston Milton Halt opened on 3 July 1933 between Worle Junction and Weston super Mare to serve a growing suburb. It was unusual in

4-4-0 No 3818 *County of Radnor* just arrived at Platform 2 in the Locking Road excursion station, Weston super Mare, *c* 1924. (Author's collection)

Weston Milton Halt, view east 1 June 1966. Its components came from the Taunton concrete works. (Author)

The exterior of the up side of Weston super Mare station, 2 September 1990. The neat frontage, spoilt by an ugly nameboard mounting, was designed by the Bristol & Exeter Railway engineer Francis Fox. (Author)

4-4-0 No 3834
County of Somerset
at Weston super
Mare with a train of
horse boxes, 12 July
1921. These engines
were uncomfortable
to ride on and were
referred to as
'Churchward's
Rough Riders'.
(M J Tozer
collection)

that some expresses called there as well as local trains. The second is the delightful 1884 through station at Weston. The architect was again Francis Fox. Building work is carried out in pale grey local stone. It has a pleasant exterior canopy and the ridge and furrow roof above the sharply-curved platforms is impressive. It is supported on decorated lattice girders and the tapered columns are embellished with a spiral design at the base and acanthus leaves on the capitals.

At Weston was an attractive stone-built engine shed that closed in August 1960. In 1947 its allocation was one shunting engine and two express engines. As an economy measure the track on either side of Weston General station was singled on 31 January 1972.

The Dunball Wharf Line

From Dunball station a line led to Dunball Wharf on the River Parrett. At one time the ½-mile line dealt with a considerable trade in molasses and the wharf was colloquially known as 'Dunball Treacle Mines'. Its history started back in May 1836 when the Bristol & Exeter Railway was mooted and an Act authorised a branch from the main line to Dunball Wharf. The company, however, had spent all its money on the main line and had none left with which to construct the branch.

The need for such a line was still felt so in 1844 two Bristol & Exeter directors built a private horse-worked broad gauge railway from the main line to the wharf, principally for coal traffic. The line certainly speeded fuel deliveries to Taunton and the West, as at that date there was no through rail communication between South Wales and the West of England except via Gloucester.

The opening of the wharf line meant that coal could be shipped from South Wales and the Forest of Dean to Dunball and from there distributed by rail.

Dunball: view towards Bridgwater *c* 1910. The wharf branch curves away, right. By the side of the signal box a wagon turntable gives access to a cement works, the siding crossing the main line at right-angles. (M J Tozer collection)

Some shipowners diverted their craft from Bridgwater Docks, then without a rail connection, and thus the railway was now competing with the Bridgwater & Taunton Canal and the Grand Western Canal for coal traffic. Consumers benefited as the cost of rail transport for coal from Dunball to Tiverton fell from 4s 9d a ton in 1851 to 1s 3d a ton in the following year.

In 1867 the Bristol & Exeter was authorised by an Act of Parliament to purchase and extend Dunball Wharf and convert the line from a horse-worked into a locomotive-worked branch. Rebuilding the line was completed and the first steam train ran over it in November 1869. The branch was mixed gauge so that it could carry either broad or standard gauge rolling stock. The extension of the wharf itself was finished in 1874. Between 1876 and 1881 the wharf dealt with about 100,000 tons of traffic annually, but after that quantities declined, especially following the opening of the Severn Tunnel when so much of the South Wales trade was transferred to rail. Nevertheless, a daily coal train still ran from Dunball to Exeter, remaining broad gauge until final conversion in May 1892.

The wharf dealt with timber, sand, gravel, cement and molasses. There was also an animal feedstuffs distribution depot of Messrs J Bibby and an Esso petroleum depot which off-loaded supplies brought by barge across the Channel from the Milford Haven refinery.

Speed over the branch was restricted to 5 mph and special regulations were in force for crossing the A38 – a man with a red flag was required to bring

A United Molasses rail tank wagon at Dunball Wharf, 1 June 1966. (Author)

road traffic to a halt and loads were limited to a maximum of 25 wagons when the engine was propelling the train. The line from the station to the wharf was 792yd in length and had a weighbridge for measuring the weight of railway wagons and their contents.

The short line was only capable of taking the smallest GWR shunting engine and it was stabled at Bridgwater. One of the interesting engines to work the line was No 2194 *Kidwelly* that the GWR inherited when it took over the Burry Port & Gwendraeth Valley Railway in South Wales. Another locomotive seen on the line was No 1338 owned by the Cardiff Railway, the only engine from that company to stray so far from home under GWR ownership which could proudly claim that, when withdrawn in September 1963, it was the last Cardiff Railway engine remaining in the service of British Railways. The Dunball Wharf branch closed on 22 April 1967.

The Bridgwater Docks Branch

When the Bristol & Exeter Railway opened, Bridgwater Corporation joined its wharf on the River Parrett to the main line by means of a horse-worked line called the 'Communication Works'. It opened in 1845 and was leased to the Bristol & Exeter in 1859. In 1866 a public meeting in the town unanimously approved the purchase of the Bridgwater & Taunton Canal by the Bristol & Exeter and their proposal to extend the wharf line by means of a telescopic bridge to the docks. At the same time the existing line was to be converted to mixed gauge and made suitable for locomotive operation. The bridge was opened in March 1871. It was divided into three sections and to open it the signals at each end were placed at danger and a steel arm locked across the rails, physically preventing trains from trying to pass. Gates across the footbridge and rail track were locked. Safety precautions thus completed, the first section of the bridge moved sideways, on wheels running on special rails, into a space. The second section, spanning most of the river, was moved lengthways into the space

Part of the railway-owned Bridgwater Docks, 8 October 1966. A GWR steam crane built in 1901 is on the far right. (Author)

vacated by the first section, thus allowing ships to pass. The third section remained fixed. The bridge sections were moved by power from a stationary steam engine. In 1913, when the engine working the bridge failed, it was imperative that the spans be moved, so gangers opened it by hauling on ropes. As upper berths of the docks fell out of use, the bridge has not been opened since 1948.

From 1844 onwards the docks were cleaned by a Brunel-designed steam-powered boat pulling itself along on a chain dragging a scraper that drew the mud into deep-water

Simplex petrol shunter No 15 at Bridgwater Docks. Built in March 1923, it was broken up in 1951. Above the number the small letters GWR appear in the style adopted for engines taken over from absorbed companies in 1922-24. (Author's collection)

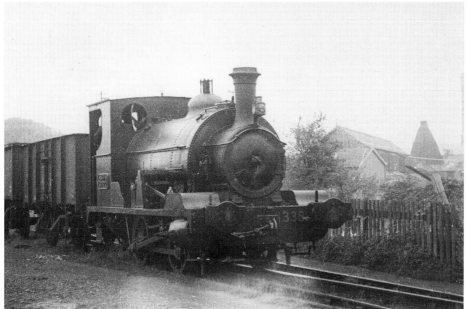

Ex-Cardiff Railway No 1338 shunting at Bridgwater Docks, 13 October 1951. (Colin Roberts)

The retractable railway bridge on the Bridgwater Docks branch, 8 October 1966. The railway bridge is immediately beyond the footbridge across the River Parrett. (Author)

The retracting bridge on the Bridgwater Docks branch: machinery in the engine house, right, moves the section of rail in the foreground to the right, leaving space into which the span beyond can be retracted, 8 October 1966. (Author)

The section of track in the foreground moves into the space, left, to allow the section of the track behind the photographer to take its place, 8 October 1966. (Author)

channels. There it was swept into the river by the flow of water. The vessel is now at the Maritime Museum, Exeter, and is the oldest working steam-powered boat in the world.

The opening of the Severn Tunnel in 1886 dealt Bridgwater shipping trade a severe blow. The narrow, winding estuary of the Parrett proved unsuitable for modern shipping, and the docks became derelict in the 1960s. Usually, small tank engines shunted at the docks but between 1932 and 1939 a Simplex petrol shunter built in 1923 was used. The docks branch closed in April 1967.

The Durston to Yeovil Branch

The single-track broad gauge line from Durston to Hendford on the outskirts of Yeovil was opened by the Bristol & Exeter on 1 October 1853. Trains first ran through to the Wilts, Somerset & Weymouth Railway station at Pen Mill on 2 February 1857. On 1 June 1861

Brunel's mud scraper at Bridgwater Docks, 8 October 1966. This vessel is preserved. (Author)

Yeovil Town Joint station was opened and the terminus at Hendford was relegated to the goods department.

Beyond Durston was Lyng Halt, opened on 24 September 1928. The platform consisted of a sleeper face with a back filling surmounted by a timber shelter. The halt closed with the withdrawal of the Durston to Yeovil passenger service on 15 June 1964. Athelney opened on 1 October 1853 as a single platform but was necessarily rebuilt in 1906 when the section became part of a new, more direct line to the West. Because of its location on an embankment both the main building on the down platform and the waiting shelter on the up were of timber. Athelney signal box can now be seen at Staverton, on the preserved South Devon railway.

Lyng Halt, 21 August 1962. (Author)

Athelney, view down 21 August 1962. After closure one of these platform buildings was purchased by the local cricket club for use as a pavilion. (Author)

East of Athelney the main line follows the course of the Yeovil line to Curry Rivel Junction where they divide. The branch line from Curry Rivel Junction to Langport West station was doubled on 2 July 1906. Langport West station consisted of a Brunel-type building on the up platform. Originally a canopy surrounded all four walls but latterly only covered the platform. The waiting shelter was sited on the down platform, which was longer than the up. The station site was very prone to flooding.

Thorney & Kingsbury Halt opened on 28 November 1927 and consisted of concrete parts cast at the GWR's Taunton works. A small office was at one end

Floods at Langport West, November 1894. (Author's collection)

No 7436 approaches Martock with a Yeovil to Taunton freight. Of the five wagons in the consist, traffic on all but one will require the use of a crane to unload. 21 August 1962. (Author)

of the timber shelter, which in turn was sheltered by an overbridge. South of the halt a siding opened on 30 September 1932 to serve Nestlé's Dairy.

The original platform at Martock with its building of Ham stone was on what became the down platform when the up platform was added. The platforms were staggered because of tracks to the busy goods yard but were connected by a footbridge.

The single-tracked Montacute station had a small stone building and the original timber platform was replaced by concrete sections that have been preserved and now form Doniford Beach Halt on the West Somerset Railway. Hendford station closed on 1 June 1861 when Yeovil Town Joint station opened. Hendford Halt, opened on 2 May 1932, was a single concrete platform sur-mounted by a timber waiting shelter. It was here that Messrs Petters, who made oil engines and also traded as Westland Aircraft Limited, had their own private siding from August 1913 until September 1965. The halt was used by its workers.

In 1867 the standard gauge Somerset & Dorset Railway planned to con-struct a branch to Bridgwater. That would have been in direct competition with the broad gauge Bristol & Exeter, so in order to offer an alternative to the proposed London & South Western and Somerset & Dorset branch and thus avoid compet-ition, the Bristol & Exeter paid £125,000 to lay a third rail (and so accommodate standard gauge trains) from Highbridge, where it made a junction with the Somerset & Dorset, through Bridgwater and Durston to Yeovil.

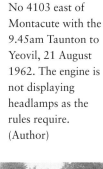

No 4103 east of Montacute with the 9.45am Taunton to Yeovil, 21 August 1962. The engine is not displaying headlamps as the rules require. (Author)

Broad gauge Bristol & Exeter Railway No 73 on the turntable at Yeovil, Pen Mill. The photograph was taken pre-1876 when it was taken over by the GWR. (Author's collection)

In 1936 a non-stop diesel railcar service was introduced over the branch on Mondays to Fridays. In the forward direction the service originated at Weymouth, affording a unique through working, while the return timing continued semi-fast to Trowbridge and stations thence to Bristol. The Yeovil to Taunton express timings showed a shaving of about 20 minutes on steam services.

During World War II the branch was designated an alternative route should the main Southern railway line between Exeter and Yeovil have become blocked. To keep Southern Railway Exmouth Junction shed crews familiar with the line, using an SR engine, they regularly worked two trains each way daily over the branch.

The Chard Branch

In 1830 some enterprising local people invited an Exeter engineer, James Green, to make a report on the feasibility of cutting a canal to link Chard with the Bridgwater & Taunton Canal. He carried out the survey but suggested that the modern idea, and a better business proposition, would be to construct a railway. His employers believed they knew best and an Act for constructing the canal was obtained three years later. It opened in 1842.

The Chard Railway Company's garter. (Author's collection)

In the Railway Mania of 1845 Chard featured in two plans for linking the English and Bristol channels. The Bridgwater & Taunton and the Chard Canal companies, alarmed at the threat of a serious loss of traffic, countered the suggestion with their own railway. Parliament refused to sanction the line but allowed a railway from Creech St Michael to Ilminster. The Chard Canal

Company immediately applied for an Act to convert its waterway from Ilminster to Chard into a railway and the Act was obtained in 1847. The Chard Canal Company changed its name to the Chard Railway Company, but as the concern was heavily in debt no funds were available actually to construct the line. Local people revived the project in 1852 and in the following year obtained an Act to convert the canal, but lack of capital again resulted in failure.

In 1859 it was proposed that a line be built from Chard to the London & South Western Railway's Exeter line, then under construction. Unfortunately the contractor failed and so did his replacement, so the standard gauge line was not opened until 8 May 1863, almost three years after the main line. Some complained that the fare of 4d for three miles was 'exhorbitant and abominable'.

Constructing an overbridge at Thornfalcon *c* 1865. (Author's collection)

The branch was worked by the London & South Western, which took over the line in 1864.

The new line only partly fulfilled the need and Chard still hankered after a rail link to Taunton. The Chard & Taunton Railway Act was obtained in 1861 but local people were unwilling to invest. In 1863 the Bristol & Exeter was granted an Act to take over the powers of the Chard & Taunton Company and build a broad gauge line.

All engineering works, including the 154yd Hatch Tunnel, were made wide enough for double track though only single was ever laid. The line opened to passengers on 11 September 1866, but as the goods sheds were incomplete, freight was not carried until the following March.

In 1878, when the Bristol & Exeter decided to convert its branches to standard gauge, it deliberately retained broad gauge on the Chard branch in order to prevent the London & South Western Railway from obtaining running powers to Taunton. When the decision was made finally to abolish the broad gauge, the 13-mile branch was converted on 19 July 1891. The task took only 20 hours. Although the conversion permitted through traffic over the branch from the London & South Western to the GWR, the demand was low. During the summer months a weekly excursion ran from Taunton to Seaton. It was formed of GWR stock and was worked on from Chard Junction station by a London & South Western engine sent from Yeovil Town shed.

On 30 December 1916 the London & South Western's Chard Town station was closed as an economy measure and from 1 January 1917 the GWR worked trains from Taunton through to Chard Junction. It is interesting to record that, as another economy measure, as early as 1896 the South Western's Chard Town station had been controlled by the GWR station master.

A report on the branch issued in 1925 revealed interesting statistics: the daily average of coal and mineral wagons sent and received was 1 and 2 respectively. Figures for wagons of general goods were 12 and 23. A total of 626 wagons of livestock was carried over the branch annually and 83,789 milk churns.

To combat bus competition halts were opened at Donyatt and Ilton on 5 and 26 May 1928 respectively. The branch offered the great potential for development as a through route between the Midlands and Lyme Regis, Seaton, Sidmouth and Exmouth, but the opportunity was never seized.

An invasion exercise near Ilminster in May 1942. The 'signal box' is actually a pill box. The engine is 0-4-2T No 5812. (Author's collection)

During World War II the Taunton the defensive stop line was constructed from the Parrett Estuary to Seaton and the line followed the Chard branch. Some of the pillboxes designed by the theatrical and film designer Oliver Messel were disguised: the one at Ilton was like a water tank and that at Ilminster a signal box.

The passenger service was suspended on 3 February 1951 because of the fuel crisis but following strong protests was re-instated on 7 May. The passenger service finally succumbed on 10 September 1962 and the goods service ended on 6 July 1964, though the line between Chard Junction and Chard Town lasted until 18 April 1966.

Branch trains left the main line at Creech Junction, having to cross all the through lines. The first station, latterly named Thornfalcon, had also been known as Thorne Falcon and later just Thorne. The station buildings were of timber and a goods loop passed, unusually and inconveniently, across the station entrance. Hatch had a Brunel-style brick station with stone doorways and windows and its chimneys were tall. Ilton Halt was very basic, having a seat but no shelter.

Ilminster station was similar to that at Hatch and only one platform was provided. Donyatt Halt had a wooden shelter. Chard Joint station was interesting. Constructed by the Bristol & Exeter in Brunel style in keeping with

Thornfalcon station 21 August 1962. The goods yard is behind the signal box. (Author)

Hatch Beauchamp station, a well-designed Brunel-style building. The chimney stacks are worth a second look. Taken c 1925 the photograph shows the station garden well maintained. In the distance is Hatch Tunnel. (Author's collection)

the other stations, it was designed with a bay platform at each end to keep broad gauge and standard gauge trains separate. One platform, which eventually became a through platform, was covered by a train shed befitting the town's status. In its early days the Bristol & Exeter and the London & South Western each had their own station masters and booking offices. The brick-built engine shed closed on 14 July 1924.

A quarter of a mile south of the station the track became part of the London & South Western and a ¼-mile branch from South Western's Chard Town joined. Chard Town had a single terminal platform and a corrugated-iron building. From the opening of Chard Joint station on 11 September 1866 the South Western trains from Chard Junction ran to Chard Town and then reversed before proceeding along the new line to Chard Joint. To avoid that time-wasting movement a platform was built on the through line close to Chard Town station. The line to the former South Western engine shed was lifted in December 1929.

The layout at Chard Junction was unusual and inconvenient. The branch platform and station were parallel with, but separate from, the main line and no direct through running was possible. Trains proceeding east had to reverse once and those going westward twice.

The London & South Western Railway's Chard Town station. A coalman is filling a 1-cwt scoop before tipping it into a sack. To his right against the goods shed wall are 1-cwt full sacks awaiting delivery. About 1960. (Author's collection)

No 3787 working the 3.15pm Taunton to Chard Junction approaches the terminus, 21 August 1962. (Author)

No 4663 at Chard Junction on the last day of passenger service, 8 September 1962. (John Cornelius)

The descent from Chard to Chard Junction was down a gradient of 1 in 80 and in the 1930s a locomotive and two coaches failed to stop at the platform, demolished the buffers and ran into the road. There was a repeat performance some twenty years later. On another occasion, when the congested goods yard at Chard Town was being shunted the crew decided, in order to get the engine at the correct end, to fly shunt the brake van and three wagons. That involved the locomotive hauling the vehicles for a short distance, uncoupling the engine, and running ahead into the siding while the shunter pulled the point lever to allow the van and wagons to roll towards the branch. Although in theory that was a time-saver, it practice it was not without risk, and so it proved that day. In attempting to step on the running board of the brake van in order to enter and apply the brake, the shunter stumbled and nearly fell. He failed to mount the van and the train ran down the gradient to Chard Junction, witnesses estimating that it reached about 40 mph before demolishing the buffer stops at the end of the bay platform, passing through a fence, crossing the road and entering the car park of the Chard Road Hotel.

The Taunton to Minehead Branch

Watchet was a very important port in the 19th century and coal could be brought easily by sea from South Wales, avoiding the long and expensive rail journey via Gloucester. Enterprising investors realised that a rail link to Watchet would be profitable. The Bristol & Exeter undertook to work the line and pay the West Somerset Railway 55% of the gross receipts with a guarantee of £4500 *per annum*. The West Somerset Railway engineer was Brunel and it proved to be one of his last undertakings. The ceremonial opening was on 29 March 1862 and to the general public on 31 March. At first the line could only be used by passengers because the goods sheds were not ready until August. It quickly proved popular. In July 1863 800 excursionists travelled from Bristol to Watchet in a 27-coach train hauled from Taunton by two engines. On 1 September the same year a special 15-coach excursion was run from Taunton to Watchet carrying 1000 passengers for a boat trip to Ilfracombe. Unfortunately one of the three steamers to carry them onwards failed to materialise and 300 of the trippers had to remain at Watchet.

R P Brereton, a pupil of Brunel, was engineer for the extension of the line from Watchet to Minehead. The Minehead Railway was relatively easy to construct apart from a rock cutting at Bilbrook that was ¾ mile long with a maximum depth of 37ft. Earth slippages caused delays. In September 1872 a new German explosive called 'Lithofracteur' was used in the cutting. Designed to be safe to transport and store, it could only be fired by a special detonator. As its explosive power was twelve times greater than gunpowder, smaller holes could be drilled in the rock. The ruling gradient of the extension was 1 in 65, quite steep for a railway. During construction serious labour problems arose and at one point navvies were only kept out of the office of the clerk of works by a loaded revolver. The 8¼ miles of broad gauge line were opened on 16 July 1874.

With the opening to Minehead, Watchet locomotive shed, turntable and water tower were moved to the new terminus. Four days after the extension was opened, the first excursion arrived carrying 800 employees of Bristol Wagon Works in 15 coaches. A poor impression was made; they were drunk, stole from shops, spoilt gardens and were rude to people. Between Dunster and Minehead the line was raised on an embankment 4ft above the land, but even so on 13 November 1875 the line was inundated by the sea. A similar thing happened on 8 October 1960 and the rail service between Blue Anchor and Minehead had to be suspended and replaced with buses.

With hindsight it seems odd that the Minehead extension was built to the broad gauge because the entire branch was converted to standard gauge on Sunday 29 October 1882. As many as 500 men in 7 gangs of 70 worked with such vigour that soon after midday a standard gauge special was able to reach Minehead. The following day one passenger train ran in each direction, and on Tuesday morning the normal service was resumed.

The Minehead Railway was taken over by the GWR in 1897 after that company had acquired all its capital. The GWR had to reach its possession over West Somerset Railway metals, for the latter retained independence until 1922.

In the 1930s, for about six Sundays in the spring, a Holiday Haunts Express was run from Bath, Bristol and Weston super Mare to Watchet, Dunster and Minehead. Sufficient time was given to passengers to book their apartments for a longer visit later in the season. Fares for the special train varied from 5s to 10s. The GWR started camp coaches in 1934, one of the first at Blue Anchor. Passengers purchasing railway tickets to the station could hire the coach for accommodation for a very reasonable sum.

The opening of Butlin's holiday camp at Minehead in 1962 increased the summer passenger traffic and as many as 2000 long-distance passengers were

Diesel-hydraulic D7017, now preserved on the West Somerset Railway, at Bishop's Lydeard working the 10.00am Taunton to Minehead, 8 June 1963. (Author)

A diesel multiple-unit enters Bishop's Lydeard with the 9.05am Minehead to Taunton, 8 June 1963. (Author)

hauled on a peak summer Saturday. From 26 February 1968 economies were made on the branch when, except at terminal stations, passengers obtained their tickets from the conductor-guard. Even so, the line was not found to be economic and the last train ran on 2 January 1971.

Fortunately, enthusiasts were anxious for the line to continue. The first section of the preserved West Somerset Railway was re-opened between Minehead and Blue Anchor on 28 March 1976, eventually reaching Bishop's Lydeard on 9 June 1979. It has proved a very popular line and is important to the area's economy.

Norton Fitzwarren, although the actual junction, was not served by express trains and most passengers were exchanged at Taunton. Bishop's Lydeard, the first station on the branch, has typical, economic buildings on the original single platform and an adjacent, relatively large goods shed. A second platform opened on 2 July 1906. During World War I King George V and Queen Mary spent the night in the Royal Train in the goods yard. All coal was removed and the yard decorated with flowers. In 1943 a Ministry of Works siding served a food depot. A United States' military hospital was nearby and ambulance trains brought the wounded following the D-Day Normandy landings in 1944. In addition to the usual traffic for a country station, Bishop's Lydeard also despatched sugar beet and rabbits.

A particularly poignant accident occurred in 1874 when the Bristol & Exeter decided to install a new crane in the goods yard. Fred Mantel, son of a

permanent way packer, played in the pit dug for its foundations. It had flooded and the cold weather caused it to develop a thin layer of ice. Fred fell through the ice, was unable to climb out and was found drowned.

Crowcombe (Crowcombe Heathfield until 1 December 1889) reverted to its original name in 1992. It had a single platform with a small, low stone building until 1879 when a down platform was constructed. At one time an overhead cableway brought stone from Triscombe Quarry crushing plant to the GWR siding. In 1931 7000 tons of stone were sent away by rail.

The station master lived in a house 200yd north of the station and it was one of the daily tasks of the lad porter to hand-pump water from the station well to the house. It took over an hour.

No 4160 at Bishop's Lydeard on the preserved West Somerset Railway, working the 12.20pm to Minehead, 30 July 1996. (Author)

The down platform at Bishop's Lydeard seen from the fireman's side of the cab of No 4160. Notice the fire irons on top of the side tank and the 'mushroom' ventilator to let air escape when the tank is filled. Milk churns on the platform help create the scene of yesteryear. (Author)

In 1964 the station was used by the Beatles when filming 'A Hard Day's Night'. The station also featured in the BBC's 'The Lion, the Witch and the Wardrobe' and also the film 'Land Girls'.

Leigh Wood level crossing was where in 1913 one of the very few women was concerned in traffic operations on a British railway. When employed by the GWR at Chard in 1880 Mrs Hill's husband met with a serious accident. He was transferred to the relatively light job of gatekeeper at Leigh Wood. In the event he was never again fit for duty. His wife therefore undertook his work and carried it out so efficiently that, after his death in 1881, she was allowed to remain in charge. Beyond is Leigh Bridge loop, opened on 16 July 1933 to shorten the single line section between Crowcombe and Williton.

Stogumber, because of its position on an embankment, had its single platform and waiting shelter on the down side, quite separate from the ground level station building on the opposite side of the track. The station, although apparently insignificant, belied its appearance. It was closer to Crowcombe village than Crowcombe station and sold more tickets annually than Bishop's Lydeard, Crowcombe and Dunster.

Although some mocked British Railways, it looked after its customers. When T H Besley, the Stogumber fishmonger, heard that the station was to be reduced to a halt he was greatly concerned as he received consignments of fish daily on the early morning train. He was also anxious as to whether the handcart could still be made available to him to transport his boxes along the platform. Only four days after writing he received a reply saying that the guard would put out his consignment of fish and obtain his signature before the train started. He would be allowed to purchase the handcart in return for a 10-shilling postal order. British Railways omitted to say that it considered the cart too old for further use and it would only have been scrapped if returned to Swindon.

Williton had but a single platform until 1874 when an up platform was added. The signal box is the only one of Bristol & Exeter design still extant, and furthermore is in working order. The nearby Doniford Brook was prone to flooding the station. Williton enjoyed a fortnightly cattle market, after which many animals were despatched by rail. Some 10,000 tons of timber were also sent away annually. Even in 1959 13,500 tickets were sold in the booking office.

Doniford Beach Halt opened on 27 June 1987. The station office block at Watchet is odd inasmuch as it is set at right angles to the platform because the station was originally the line's terminus. It is curious that, although the principal intermediate station on the branch, it has just one platform. In June 1907 a corrugated-iron pagoda shelter was placed towards the east end of the platform to give additional waiting accommodation. Esparto grass was an important import at Watchet Harbour and when a vessel arrived about 350 railway wagons were required for its transport. Open wagons carrying esparto grass and wood pulp required sheeting, no easy task because a tarpaulin weighed about 1 cwt.

Blue Anchor signalman Martin Southwood holds the Blue Anchor to Williton single line staff for the fireman to collect. With his other hand he will receive the Dunster to Blue Anchor staff. The bunker of No 4277 is in the foreground and also the handle of the oil lamp, 19 September 1996. (Author)

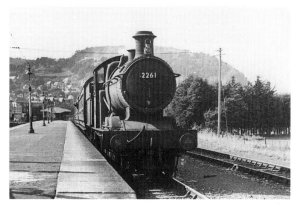

(Left) 2-8-0 No 48773 crossed the ungated level crossing at Dunster heading, tender-first, the 14.10 Bishop's Lydeard to Minehead, 13 August 1993. The star below the number indicates that the driving wheels are balanced for working a fitted freight train. In World War II this locomotive served in the Sudan. (Author)

(Right) No 2261 leaves Minehead with a train to Taunton, 24 August 1950. (Revd Alan Newman)

Minehead c 1880. Unlike the situation at many resorts, the station is very close to the beach. The loaded coach and four is probably destined for Lynmouth. Seven bathing machines are on the beach. (Author's collection)

Leaving Watchet, the line passes Watchet Paper Mills, crosses the West Somerset Mineral Railway and runs beside it for 1½ miles. Kentsford loop opened on 10 July 1933 to break up the long section between Williton and Blue Anchor.

Washford has only a single platform. Its cattle market was on the first Monday in the month and used 20-30 cattle wagons each market day, the station dealing with more cattle than any other on the branch. Beyond, the line descends at 1 in 65 through Bilbrook Cutting.

The original station at Blue Anchor was deliberately spartan in style as it was intended for artisans and their families, while their betters would patronise Minehead. A crossing loop and a new down platform opened on 5 January 1904 with a standard brick waiting shelter. North of the line immediately after Sea Lane Crossing was Ballasto (ballast hole) Field from where the line's original ballast was extracted.

The single platform at Dunster has an impressive entrance to its stone building because the Luttrell family at Dunster Castle were promoters of the Minehead Railway. In the 1920s and 1930s polo tournaments were held at the Castle and ponies arrived in special trains, sometimes consisting of over 20 horseboxes. There was a Shell-Mex depot at the station and an average of 17 wagons of pit props were despatched weekly. From 19 March 1934 the track from Dunster to Minehead was doubled.

Minehead station originally only had one platform. A second was added in 1905 when the original was lengthened. In 1934 it was lengthened still further and was capable of holding a 16-coach train. The goods yard dealt with general merchandise.

Minehead station 1923. The booking office for the Lynton horse-drawn coach is on the left, just inside the first gate. Notice the very large corrugated-iron pagoda housing the parcels office and cloakroom. Advertisements include those for Nestlé's milk, Admiralty serges, Whitbread stout, Petter's oil engines and Robertson's marmalade. The goods wagon on the left contains roped and sheeted timber. As the load overhangs, a runner wagon is used – in this case a London & North Western Railway coal wagon belonging to the locomotive department and not the traffic department. (Author's collection)

Norton Fitzwarren to Dulverton

The broad gauge Devon & Somerset Railway between Norton Fitzwarren and Barnstaple was beset by many vicissitudes. By August 1866 the route had been staked out from Norton Fitzwarren to Wiveliscombe but that month the contractor, Messrs Pickering, was forced to discharge his men as the Devon & Somerset Railway was unable to pay for the work done. Construction soon resumed, but towards the end of August two navvies fell ill with cholera and in an effort to prevent it spreading, pitch fires were lit in every street. The Devon & Somerset failed to pay Messrs Pickering on 29 September 1866 and construction was suspended until 11 May 1870 when the contract was given to John Langham Reed. On 8 June 1871 the line opened from Norton Fitzwarren to Wiveliscombe. Work continued on the rest of the line, major engineering works in Somerset being Bathealton Tunnel of 445yd, Venn Cross Viaduct of 159 yd, and Venn Cross Tunnel of 246yd. It opened on 1 November 1873 and was worked by the Bristol & Exeter. The last broad gauge train ran over the line on Saturday 14 May 1881; the line was converted 15 – 17 May and a standard gauge goods and two passenger trains ran on 18 May. Thereafter the full service operated.

One interesting train on the line was the daily rabbit special from South Molton, but myxomatosis brought an end to that traffic. The branch closed on 3 October 1966.

Milverton station had a brick twin-pavilion building on its platform. An up platform was added in 1880, its timber waiting shelter of typical Bristol & Exeter

Milverton, view down *c* 1879 in broad gauge days before the line was doubled. Notice the disc and crossbar signal at danger. Beside it is the flag signal for 'Caution'. (Author's collection)

design with delightful bargeboards identical to those at Axbridge on the Cheddar Valley line. Wiveliscombe station was of similar, though superior, design in stone, its booking office having an attractive bay window on the platform side.

Bathealton Tunnel, on a rising gradient, caused problems to locomotive crews. One engine hauling a passenger train slipped to a standstill with the driver and fireman overcome by fumes. On regaining consciousness they found that they were out of the tunnel and rolling backwards towards Wiveliscombe. They stopped the train, made another attempt to climb through the tunnel, and that time succeeded. Drivers tried various techniques when approaching the tunnel. Some sanded the rails before entering, but as there was a curve before the tunnel portal the train's progress was retarded. Other drivers took their chance and did

Milverton *c* 1910, following the addition of the crossing loop *c* 1880. Signalling permitted a down goods train on the right hand line to be overtaken by a down passenger train using the left hand line. (Author's collection)

Venn Cross Viaduct, 159yd in length, spanning the River Tone. (Author's collection)

not apply sand unless their engine slipped. At least one driver always sanded just the straight rail before the tunnel and never experienced any problems.

Venn Cross Viaduct was insufficiently strong to support the weight of two engines unless a tender separated them. Thus, if a tank engine was piloting a tender engine, the tank engine had to be uncoupled and run over the viaduct first before being re-coupled on the other side. Should the second engine have been working tender-first there was no problem, though tender-first working was disliked by crews as it was cold and draughty and coal dust blew in their faces.

In 1944, just before D-Day, certain railway locations were guarded as it was believed that the enemy might destroy them in order to delay the invasion. Venn Cross Viaduct was protected by the Home Guard. On one single day in May 1944 no less than 15 troop trains arrived at Dulverton, each carrying 1000 men and vast stores of food.

The line emerged from Venn Cross Tunnel into Venn Cross station, 666ft above sea level. The original platform was on the down side. Although most of the station was in Somerset, the west end of the platform and the goods shed were in Devon. A second platform was added in April 1905. The next two

Venn Cross station 25 August 1953. The station buildings are at the top of the embankment behind the signal box. In the distance is the 246yd Venn Cross Tunnel. (Dr A J G Dickens)

No 6323 derailed
east of Dulverton
following a brake
failure. (Tony
Harvey)

A busy time at
Dulverton station:
No 6346 arrives
with a Taunton to
Barnstaple stopping
train; the Exe Valley
train to Exeter,
centre; while the
engine of a
Barnstaple to
Taunton train is
right. (T J Saunders)

stations, Morebath and Morebath Junction Halt, were in Devon, but Dulverton
was in Somerset. It was the most important intermediate station on the line and
always had two platforms; a third was added in1902 to cope with the Exe Valley
service from Exeter via Tiverton. The up platform at Dulverton had a station
master's house in addition to a single-story stone-built station office.

6 Broad Gauge Lines: The Wilts, Somerset & Weymouth Railway

THE WILTS, Somerset & Weymouth Railway was planned to link the GWR near Chippenham with Weymouth, branches serving Devizes, Radstock and Salisbury, while a line from Bathampton joined the main route just east of Bradford on Avon. It received its Act in 1845 but because of the slump following Railway Mania investment was slow. The first part in Somerset, a single line from Westbury to Frome, opened on 7 October 1850 and the mineral line to Radstock on 14 November 1854. Frome to Yeovil opened on 1 September 1856 and Weymouth was finally reached on 20 January 1857. Bradford Junction to Bathampton opened on 2 February 1857. The line was converted to standard gauge between 18 and 22 June 1874.

The broad gauge permanent way chiefly consisted of rails on longitudinal sleepers connected by transoms at intervals of 11ft. That design lent itself to fairly easy conversion as the transoms could be cut to suit the narrower gauge and the longitudinal sleepers with rails attached, slewed over to the new gauge. The actual work of conversion could be eased by previously clearing away the ballast and marking the transoms ready for cutting.

The platelayers engaged on conversion were drafted in from other districts and were carried on special trains. They received 1s 3d a day for rations and drank oatmeal and water sweetened with sugar. That gave them strength to carry out their arduous task. The GWR provided sheds for the men to sleep in and straw to sleep on, but little rest was taken, 17 or 18 hours being worked out of every 24, for the work was deliberately undertaken during long summer days.

The previous evening all broad gauge rolling stock was removed from sidings and each station master was required to provide a certificate that his station and district was clear of broad gauge stock. Much of it was eventually broken up at Swindon, though the locomotives were sold for conversion to stationary boilers.

To cope with increasing traffic, the line was doubled in 1881. In 1935 it saw some of the first diesel trains in England, but full dieselisation did not come until 6 April 1959. Until 26 September 1959 the Channel Islands boat express ran daily every summer from Paddington to Weymouth Quay while daily services ran to Wolverhampton and Bristol. Much of the Channel Islands market garden produce was also carried over the line – in 1912 124 special potato trains ran between 1 May and 24 June earning £19,062. Five tomato specials ran daily at the height of the season, while in coal-burning days the Royal Naval ships at Portland required fuelling. With the withdrawal of Channel Islands boat expresses from the route and also the market garden produce train, the line was used less intensively. Castle Cary to Yeovil was reduced to single track on 12 May 1968 and the intermediate stations at Sparkford and Marston Magna were closed on 3 October 1966. A former main line was reduced to mere branch status.

In 2002 the former Wilts, Somerset & Weymouth Railway south of Castle Cary was very much a Cinderella line, but in recent years successful regeneration has occurred. Known as the 'Heart of Wessex Line', it is supported by various highly active groups. Volunteer supporters maintain station gardens to make the environment more attractive. Others produce and distribute simple, local timetables, or arrange guided walks from the stations. Celebrations are arranged to commemorate significant dates such as the centenary of the opening of

A 'Metro' tank engine works a down stopping train calling at Frome c 1900. Notice the milk churns on the left. (A Church collection)

Avoncliff Halt or 150 years of Bradford on Avon or Yeovil Pen Mill stations. Local and county councils have been most supportive. All those efforts have succeeded in doubling the number of passengers using the line since 2002.

Freshford is the only station on the Bathampton to Bradford Junctions section of the line that stands in Somerset. Built on a curve, the cant proved a problem for less agile passengers who experienced problems with a 2-ft gap between platform and coaches on a southbound train. The problem began in 1988 when the track was re-aligned to allow passing trains to operate at a higher speed. The necessary renovation work cost £350,000 and the station was officially re-opened on 5 May 2006. To the north of the station were exchange sidings for the Limpley Stoke and Camerton branch.

The splendid Frome station has a train shed designed by Brunel's assistant J B Hannaford. The whole building is of timber and still exists today listed Grade II. In its heyday the station had a staff averaging about 45. A small locomotive shed opened in 1890 but had an allocation of 11 engines in 1947. It closed in September 1963. The opening of the shorter line to the West in 1906 brought more trains through Frome and caused it to become a bottleneck. That was in due course relieved by the opening of the avoiding line on 2 January 1933. As a result trains could avoid the 30-mph speed restriction, so the Frome cut-off saved at least ½ ton of coal each day, quite apart from reducing wear and tear on locomotives and rolling stock.

No 4636, another 0-6-0PT and two 'Prairie' tank engines stand at Frome locomotive shed. Notice the 'devil' beside the water column. This was lit in frosty weather. (Author's collection)

Witham became a junction when the East Somerset Railway was opened in 1858. With its rise in status it was give a branch platform covered by a train shed about one coach in length. From 9 June 1958 the word 'Somerset' was added to its name to distinguish it from the Essex Witham. The station closed on 9 September 1963.

Strap Lane Halt opened on 18 July 1932 with two timber platforms each with a small wooden shelter. It closed was closed from 6 October 1941 until 16 December 1946 as a World War II economy measure and finally closed on 5 June 1950.

Bruton had a typical Wilts, Somerset & Weymouth-style station. Apart from the town traffic, it was used extensively by pupils of King's School, Sunny Hill

Bruton station 23 April 1963. Beyond the footbridge is the goods shed and signal box. This side of the goods shed are the cattle pens. (Author)

The cast-iron gentlemen's urinal at Castle Cary, 27 April 1963. (Author)

School for Girls and Sexey's School for boys. The station was reduced to halt status on 6 October 1969. Today the station sees its greatest use when the Glastonbury Festival is held at Pilton.

Castle Cary became a junction when the new route to the West opened in 1906 and the building on the up platform was extended. In February 1985 the down platform was rebuilt to the island pattern to enable Weymouth trains to call at either face. On 3 September 1942 four bombs fell on the station building, killing six people and destroying 0-6-0PT No 1729. The signal box was replaced on 27 October 1942 by Messrs McAlpine using Evercreech bricks.

Sparkford had a single stone building. War Department sidings at the north end of the station opened on 28 May 1944 and were lifted by 1963 while dairy sidings at the other end of the station opened in 1932 and closed on 8 December 1963. The station itself closed on 3 October 1966.

The Millfield School special train terminating at Castle Cary station in April 1976. It is hauled by a 'Western' class diesel-hydraulic. The flat-roofed signal box is a replacement for its predecessor, destroyed by a bomb in World War II. (W H Harbor)

Sparkford station, 22 July 1966. All track in the goods yard has been lifted. (Author)

Cedric Talbot in Sparkford signal box, 1936. (W Talbot)

Marston Magna had just a single platform until the line was doubled in 1881. The station was lit by oil lamps until its closure on 3 October 1966. On 16 December 1940 a large ammunition depot was opened, initially run by the Royal Engineers but latterly by United States' troops, sited east of the station. The depot was particularly active around D-Day. The sidings were taken out of use on 5 November 1962.

Yeovil Pen Mill has a building of beautiful, honey-coloured Ham stone and until 1934 an overall roof similar to that at Frome. When the line from Castle Cary was singled in May 1968 Yeovil retained its double track and became a passing place. The timber-built engine shed closed on 5 January 1959. In 1947 it had an allocation of 10 locomotives. South of the station the line passes into Dorset.

The Radstock Branch

The broad gauge Frome to Radstock mineral branch opened on 14 November 1854, by which time the Wilts, Somerset & Weymouth Railway had been taken over by the GWR.

North of Frome station a triangular junction offered access to and from both Westbury and Castle Cary. Somerset Quarry Siding, 2 miles west of Frome, was initially served by a narrow gauge line, but in 1943 a standard gauge line through the highly picturesque Vallis Vale linked it with Whatley Quarry. From 1947 quarry trains were worked by interesting vertical-boilered Sentinel locomotives, the small boiler actually located in the cab. Later, those engines were converted to diesel-hydraulic operation.

A rural idyll: Roads Reconstruction vertical-boilered Sentinel No 1 brings a train of loaded ballast wagons to the junction with the Frome to Radstock line, 5 November 1968. (Author)

A vertical-boilered Sentinel at the Roads Reconstruction Ltd's Hapsford Quarry, 20 July 1954. This engine was exhibited at the 1925 Wembley Exhibition. (Revd Alan Newman)

Roads Reconstruction Sentinel No 3 at Whatley Quarry, 9 May 1959. The internal-use side tipping wagons look period pieces and have brakes on one side only. (Revd Alan Newman)

Two Rolls-Royce diesel locomotives coupled back to back leave Whatley Quarry in May 1972. These locomotives were rebuilt from the Sentinel vertical-boilered locomotives. (WH Harbor)

Roads Reconstruction No 2 in the picturesque Vallis Vale, 3 April 1956. Fire irons rest on a rack above the buffers. The large buffers are to prevent buffer interlocking on the line's severe curves. The flat-bottomed track is spiked directly to the sleepers. (Author)

In the early 1960s the line was modified to enable British Railway wagons to work through to the quarry to avoid transhipment of stone from internal-use wagons. In 1973 a 1½-mile deviation was built, involving three new tunnels totalling 649yd, to enable British Rail locomotives to run to Whatley Quarry. The new line was opened on 9 September 1974. In 1990 the quarry owners, Amey Roadstone Corporation, bought four General Motors diesel locomotives and named them after local villages. They were crewed by British Rail for running over Nationalised lines.

Mells Road station opened on 4 March 1887, 12 years after the Frome to Radstock line had opened to passenger traffic. It became a halt on 17 September 1956 and closed to passengers on 2 November 1959 and to goods on 15 June 1964. The station architecture was similar to that of the Bristol & North Somerset Railway.

From the station the 2-mile Newbury Railway led to Mells Colliery, Vobster Quarry and Newbury Colliery. Originally constructed to the broad gauge, it was converted in 1874. The line was horse-worked from its opening in 1857 until locomotives were introduced about 1900. The three users formed a committee and normally each undertaking used its own locomotive, but if one failed the committee's traffic manager arranged for the other two engines to cover the roster. Newbury Colliery closed in 1927, Mells in 1943; stone ceased to be hauled from Vobster about 1966. The line continued to give access to a bitumen terminal until traffic ceased about 1978.

On the approach to Radstock were Kilmersdon Colliery Sidings. The colliery itself was about ½ mile to the south and set well above the main line. The standard gauge railway from the pit ran to the head of a 500ft inclined plane set on a gradient of 1 in 8. From 10 September 1929 until closure in 1973 a Peckett 0-4-0ST worked the line. It pushed five or six wagons over the weighbridge so that a bill of lading could be written, an orange light indicating when the next wagon should be moved to the weighbridge. When the task was complete the engine pushed the wagons over an ungated level crossing, through a shallow

View up the incline towards Kilmersdon Colliery, 6 June 1968. A wagon stands at the top ready to descend. An inverted runaway wagon is on the left. The points are sprung so that the descending loaded wagon is turned to the left hand track. Notice the cable in the foreground. (Author)

Permanent way maintenance work on the Kilmersdon Colliery incline. A rake of empty wagons stands at the foot of the incline, 6 June 1968. (Author)

Nelson Loader has his hands on the levers controlling the wagons' speed on the incline, 6 June 1968. Notice the point lever on his right. Here the ascending wagon uses the right hand track. A telephone in the cabinet, left, gives communication with the man at the foot of the incline. (Author)

cutting and on to an embankment with fields on either side. To prevent wagons and the locomotive accidentally plunging down the incline, a metal stop block was placed across the rails.

A Bristol-built Peckett 0-4-0ST shunts near the head of the incline, 6 June 1968. Now named *Kilmersdon*, it is preserved on the West Somerset Railway at Washford. (Author)

The first wagon was uncoupled and hooked to a wire cable which passed round a horizontal winding drum and led down to the foot of the incline where it was attached to an empty wagon. When everything was ready, the warning bell was rung, the stop block moved aside and the loaded wagon descended, dragging up the empty, the two crossing midway.

At the head of the incline two levers controlled hand brakes on the drum in the winding house. Immediately the ascending empty wagon reached the head of the incline, a lever was pulled to place the stop block across the rails, the wagon shunted into a siding and another loaded wagon pushed to the incline head. Meanwhile the first loaded wagon at the foot of the incline had had its brakes applied just before the rope stopped, so that it was slack, hung loosely

Radstock locomotive shed, 30 March 1983. It closed to locomotives in 1929. (Author)

and could be easily uncoupled. The wagon then rolled by gravity round a sharp curve to a siding parallel with, but at a lower level than, the Frome branch. In the 1960s about 50 loaded wagons were removed daily.

Nearer Radstock was Ludlow's Colliery served by a broad gauge branch from 1854. For 90 years the yard was shunted by horses, but early in 1953 the surface was adapted to permit shunting by road tractor equipped with

A tractor adapted to shunt railway wagons seen at Marcroft's Wagon Works, Radstock, 3 July 1975. (Author's collection)

buffer beams and wagon couplings. On 19 March the colliery closed.

Radstock engine shed was opened in 1866 and closed in 1929.

Witham to Wells

The broad gauge East Somerset Railway opened from Witham to Shepton Mallet on 9 November 1858 and was extended to Wells on 1 March 1862. When in 1874 it was asked to convert to standard gauge, the capital was not available and the company had to sell to the GWR on 2 December 1874. In association with the Wilts, Somerset & Weymouth Railway, conversion was carried out between 18 and 22 June 1874. The line closed to passengers on 9 September 1963 but the eastern end of the branch was brought into intensive use from 1970 when Foster Yeoman developed Merehead stone quarry. At Cranmore David Shepherd formed the Cranmore Railway Company to trade under the name of the East Somerset Railway to preserve locomotives and rolling stock. The next phase was the granting of charity status when the new East Somerset Railway Company Limited bought the majority of David Shepherd's assets at Cranmore. In due course the line was re-opened to Mendip Vale.

From Witham the branch climbs and here gravity was put to good use. To release an engine of an up train, the empty passenger coaches were shunted back up the incline and after the engine had been uncoupled and moved to another road the coaches were allowed to gravitate back to the bay platform.

Wanstrow station was opened on 1 January 1860 but the cost of construction could not be afforded by the impecunious East Somerset Railway and was, instead, paid for by the local inhabitants. At first a small stone shelter was provided on a very short platform that was later extended. It was unstaffed until

No 5523 at Witham having arrived with the 7.58am from Yatton, 22 August 1957. Notice the train shed. A main line train, providing a connecting service, is on the left. To the left of the GWR monogram on the footbridge is the date of its construction, 1890. To the right of the locomotive's buffer beam is the cattle dock. (Author)

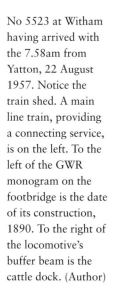

Wanstrow station
c 1895. (Author's
collection)

1 April 1909 when the first station master was appointed and a timber office erected for him. The post was Grade 6, the lowest class, yet it was the ambition of nearly every porter on the branch to become station master at Wanstrow. On 3 January 1927 a goods loop to hold 10 wagons was opened beyond the platform and dealt with coal, cattle food and livestock.

The line climbed to Merehead Quarry Siding, in use from 14 March 1948 until 30 April 1970, and was used by rail tank wagons carrying bitumen to a factory that pulverised stone and made tiles and similar products. From 16 September 1973 a chord line left the main line before reaching the site of Merehead Quarry Siding and served the new Merehead Quarry and the maintenance shed for Foster Yeomen's locomotives.

Cranmore station originally had one platform and a limestone office building, but a down platform was brought into use on 1 June 1880. The present

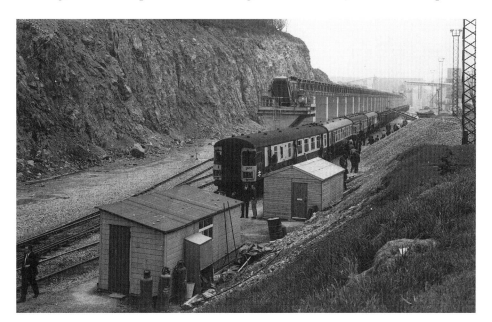

A diesel multiple-unit
at Merehead Quarry
having brought a
train load of visitors,
April 1972. (W H
Harbor)

Cranmore station,
22 August 1957.
(Author)

The 2ft gauge
Gamecock, built by
Peckett's, 1904, *en
route* to Cranmore
Quarry. (Author's
collection)

Mixed gauge track,
2ft and 4ft 8½in,
between Cranmore
and Cranmore
Quarry. (Author's
collection)

East Somerset Railway has considerably extended the building. From 1926 until 1946 when Waterlip Quarry was closed, four long sidings handled about 100 wagons of stone daily. Cranmore has a long tradition of dealing with bitumen traffic and represents a curious reversal of the business for at one period a tramway carried Andesite from Downhead via Waterlip to the railway at Cranmore. Andesite was used on macademised roads but was no longer used from about 1925 with the invention of tarmac that solved any binding problems. Marcroft Wagons Limited had a repair depot on the site of the present reproduction GWR engine shed. Occasional traffic from the National system arrives at Cranmore today as the East Somerset Railway carries out maintenance of stock for other companies. The ESR currently runs from Cranmore to Mendip Vale and trains returning to Cranmore face a rising gradient of 1 in 56 that certainly tests a locomotive's capabilities.

Doulting Siding served a stone quarry from 1868 until 1938. From here the line descends through a steep-sided cutting that provided stone for bridge building at Cranmore and Shepton Mallet. Beyond is the present Mendip Vale station that has no road access.

Kilver Street level crossing marked the approach to Shepton Mallet. Shepton station (the suffix 'High Street' was added on 26 September 1949) originally had a single platform and a stone building until a second platform with a brick waiting shelter was opened on 8 January 1895. When the station formed the branch terminus it had an engine shed which was built at a cost of £50 but it became redundant when the line was extended to Wells and so became a goods shed. The station dealt with general freight but had an agricultural bias and also specialised in beer and roadstone.

No 92203 *Black Prince* and No 928 *Stowe* outside the reproduction GWR engine shed at Cranmore, 27 April 1974. (W H Harbor)

The fireman of No 41245 heading the 2.45pm Yatton to Witham, exchanges tablets at Shepton Mallet. No 4607 working the 3.28pm Witham to Yatton stands at the other platform, 22 August 1962. (Author)

Three miles beyond Shepton were Dulcote Quarry Sidings, opened about 1880 and closed in 1969. Blasting at the quarry was permitted within specified hours, but the firing of shots was only allowed when a railwayman had arrived from Wells with a 'blasting disc' and also the electric train staff to ensure that the line was truly closed.

The East Somerset station at Wells was 'a light and neat structure' with a glass awning. It was closed to passengers on 1 January 1878 when the GWR centralised traffic on Wells Tucker Street station. The East Somerset site continued in use for goods traffic until 13 July 1964. The formation of the line

No 2340 and No 2253 stand at Wells shed, 10 May 1951. No 2340, built in 1884, was withdrawn in June 1939 but on the outbreak of World War II was re-instated and not finally withdrawn until June 1954. Below the water tower can be seen part of the coaling crane. (Revd Alan Newman)

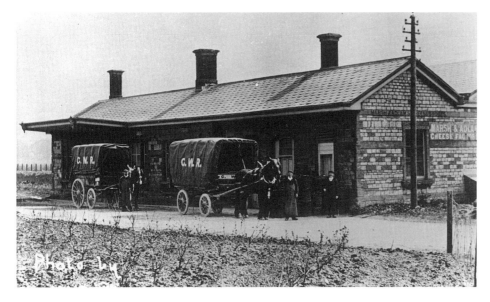

The former East Somerset Railway station at Wells in use as a store by Marsh & Adlam, cheese factors. Just visible on the far right is part of the train shed. (Author's collection)

is now used by a section of the Wells relief road named East Somerset Way. The East Somerset yard had a two-road engine shed that opened in 1874, had an allocation of two engines in 1947 and was closed in November 1963.

Castle Cary to Cogload Junction

Critics of the GWR claimed that its initials stood for 'Great Way Round' and it was certainly true that quite a few of its routes were far from beelines. It was only 15 miles from Castle Cary on the Wilts, Somerset and Weymouth Railway to Langport on the Taunton to Yeovil branch and so, for the cost of only 15 miles of line a new and shorter route to the west could be made, thus saving 20 miles over the route via Swindon and Bristol. Bridges were strengthened, the line doubled, and some of the sharper curves on the Berks and Hants Extension Railway between Reading and Stert re-aligned, while a cut-off from Stert to Westbury avoided the detour through Devizes. Castle Cary to Charlton Mackrell was opened on 1 July 1905, Somerton to Curry Rivel Junction the following 12 February; the intervening section from Charlton Mackrell to Somerton opened

Excavating the foundations for a skew bridge, Somerton, c 1904. (Author's collection)

Somerton skew
bridge, 1904.
(Author's collection)

Excavation,
Somerton, 1904.
(Author's collection)

Construction at
Somerton in 1904 on
the site of the later
goods yard.
(Author's collection)

to goods traffic on 20 May. Meanwhile, the Taunton to Yeovil branch was raised above flood level and doubled between Curry Rivel Junction and Athelney and a new line built from Athelney to Cogload Junction to avoid the detour to Durston Junction. That line opened on 2 April 1906 according to the usual practice of using goods trains on a new railway before passengers trains in order that the embankments could be compacted and any settling adjusted before faster traffic used it. Through goods trains to the West used the whole of the new line from 11 June 1906. It had been planned that express passenger trains would use it from 2 July but on 1 July a portion of Box Tunnel caved in, so the line was opened a day earlier. On 10 September 1962 stations between Athelney and Castle Cary were closed to passengers.

Extensive War Department sidings 1½ mile west of Castle Cary served Dimmer Intermediate Ammunition Depot. They were opened on 15 September 1940 and taken out of use on 8 April 1962. The sidings were widely dispersed as were each of the stores. Each structure consisted of four semi-cylindrical huts with an iron frame and double skin of corrugated iron covered in concrete. Surrounding each set of four huts was a brick blast wall.

Alford Halt opened on 21 July 1905. It was never provided with waiting shelters and another unusual feature was that ramps were only constructed at the western ends of the platforms. It closed with the withdrawal of the local passenger service on 10 September 1962.

Keinton Mandeville station comprised a principal red-brick building on the up platform and a red-brick shelter on the down, both built in the standard GWR style of the period as were all the other stations on the cut-off. Charlton Mackrell, almost identical, was a temporary terminus from its opening on 1 July 1905 until 2 July 1906. Somerton had the suffix 'Somerset' to avoid confusion with the other station of the same name in Oxfordshire on the GWR Oxford to Birmingham line. West of the station up and down loops were opened to facilitate the movement of wartime traffic. Beyond is Somerton Tunnel, 1053yd long.

Construction train at Keinton Mandeville station, 1906. The nearest wagon has wooden buffers. (Author's collection)

Putting the finishing
touches to Somerton
station, 1906.
(Author's collection)

Putting the finishing touches to Somerton station, 1906. (Author's collection)

Long Sutton & Pitney opened on 1 October 1907 as a halt in the year after the line opened to through passenger traffic. Each platform had one of the typical GWR corrugated-iron pagoda waiting shelters. The halt became a station on 6 April 1908 when the goods depot was opened. The passenger platforms were lengthened in 1914. The next station, Langport East, had particularly fine flower beds and Edwardian gentry travelled from Paddington to view peonies at the nearby Kelways Nurseries. Just over a mile to the west is the 211yd Langport Viaduct, the foundations of which were sunk 50ft through peat bog. Adjoining is a 105ft span girder bridge over the River Parrett.

At Curry Rivel Junction the branch from Yeovil came in and the track for the next 4 miles was based on the Yeovil branch widened and raised above flood level. Althelney has already been described (page 85). West of the station the single line to Durston branched from the main line. The branch was slewed northwards on 4 October 1943 to create room for up and down loops opened on 31 October 1943. Cogload Junction, where the new cut-off joined the old line from Bristol, was originally a flat junction, but when the main line through Taunton was quadrupled in the 1930s the down line from Bristol was carried over both tracks of the Castle Cary line. That 'flying junction' meant that conflicting routes were now avoided and no train could be delayed by another.

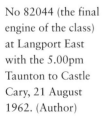

No 82044 (the final engine of the class) at Langport East with the 5.00pm Taunton to Castle Cary, 21 August 1962. (Author)

7 Standard Gauge Lines: The London & South Western Railway

THE SALISBURY & Yeovil Railway bill had a close escape from rejection. The official responsible for advertising the bill in a certain newspaper neglected to do so until the date required by Standing Orders had expired. The difficulty was cunningly surmounted by arranging with the journal's manager to print some copies of the issue containing the advertisement with an altered date, and those fraudulent copies were produced to the Examiner of Private Bills. That official, having been warned of the attempted deception, reported the matter to the House of Commons, at the same time certifying that Standing Orders had not been complied with. The newspaper manager was summoned to attend and explain his conduct, and he confessed his delinquency. To everyone's surprise, the House resolved that the Standing Orders should be dispensed with.

When the first sod was cut in 1856 the railway had only £4 5s 0d in its bank account – rather a small sum to begin construction of a line which was to cost over £½m but eventually paid its shareholders 12½%. That high figure was achieved partly because of an attractive working agreement and partly because the directors, unlike those of some other railways, avoided building feeder branches which often proved to be only expensive suckers.

The line was opened as far as Yeovil on 1 June 1860, trains terminating at the Bristol & Exeter's Hendford station. The Joint station took a further year to complete. On 18 July 1860 the line was opened through to Exeter. That day the London & South Western directors left Waterloo in a 20-coach special drawn by three engines: No 122 *Britannia*, No 151 *Montrose* and No 115 *Vulcan*, reaching Exeter seven hours later. The day was celebrated both by Exeter Fair and a total eclipse of the sun. A limited public service began the following day, full passenger services starting on 1 August and goods a month later.

The first South Western station in Somerset was Templecombe, which it later shared with the Somerset & Dorset Railway. The station was rebuilt in the 1930s. It closed on 7 March 1966 but following local pressure was re-opened on 3 October 1983, half of the signal box's upper floor becoming a booking office. Supported by the Templecombe Station Promotion Group, its gardens are a delight and well worth seeing. On the lawn is an unusual sundial erected in 1990. The small engine shed closed about 1951 and the locomotive transferred to the Somerset & Dorset shed.

No 827 passes Templecombe with a down goods. Notice the milk churns on the platform. (Author's collection)

It is a little-known fact that the South Western planned to have a water trough straddling the Dorset-Somerset border just east of Templecombe. Unlike most of the other large railway companies, the South Western did not have troughs between the rails in order that locomotives could replenish their water without stopping. In 1907 Dugald Drummond, its locomotive engineer, planned a class of engine which he believed could run non-stop from London to Exeter without the need to change engines at Salisbury. The tender of the new engine was actually built with a water pick-up apparatus, but the engine proved useless, the scheme was abandoned and the pick-up apparatus removed.

Milborne Port station was demoted to halt status on 6 November 1961 and

Four-wheeled railbus W79975 approaches Yeovil Junction from Yeovil Town, 2 April 1965. (Revd Alan Newman)

tickets were thereafter sold at the signal box. It closed on 7 March 1966. Yeovil Junction, rebuilt in 1907, has two island platforms. Sutton Bingham was architecturally different from other stations on the line. Relatively little used, it closed to passengers on 31 December

No 30182 at Yeovil Junction working the 'push-pull' service to Yeovil Town 27 August 1953. The apparatus above the leading driving wheel enables a driver to control the engine from a vestibule at the other end of the train. (Revd Alan Newman)

No 30841 passing Milborne Port on 30 June 1950 with a down goods train. The station is well off for barrows. (Author's collection)

Diesel-hydraulic D831 *Monarch* shunting milk tanks at Yeovil Junction, 15 April 1967. (Author)

An up train
approaches Sutton
Bingham station
c 1910. (Lens of
Sutton)

The entrance to
Crewkerne station
c 1905. (Author's
collection)

1962. Crewkerne was designed by the London & South Western Railways
architect Sir William Tite, M.P. for Bath, whose bust can be seen in the entrance
to the city's Guildhall. Tite's designs incorporated steep-pitched roofs. The
station is still in use. Chard Junction closed to passengers on 7 March 1966.
The nearby milk depot ceased using rail milk tanks in April 1980.

    Yeovil Town, a joint GWR and South Western station, was most impressive.
Facing the street was a long symmetrical structure in Tudor style, built of local

(Left) The main line at Chard Junction, 4 June 1976. (Author)

(Right) The rather austere building at Crewkerne station, 4 June 1976. (Author)

Yeovil Joint station c 1905. (Author's collection)

No 76067 and railbus W79975 at Yeovil Town 2 April 1965. (Revd Alan Newman)

The exterior of Yeovil Town station. Notice the ornate tops to the chimney stacks. (Author's collection)

No 30732 at Yeovil Town 27 August 1953. (Revd Alan Newman)

stone. The Bristol & Exeter and South Western each had its own booking office and station master's house. Beyond were two large glazed train sheds. The glazing gave problems and was dismantled in the early 1930s and was replaced by Southern Railway platform canopies. The station had no less than three types of platform staff: joint, Bristol & Exeter and South Western. Originally, all lines and sidings were of mixed gauge. With the withdrawal of the shuttle service from Yeovil Junction, the station closed on 2 October 1966. Adjacent to the station was a medium-sized engine shed stabling about 20 locomotives. It closed in June 1965.

No 41283 at Yeovil Town locomotive shed, 2 April 1965. This engine had a particularly interesting life. From January 1957 it was shedded at Bank Hall, Liverpool, in March 1957 it was moved to Aintree, in June that year to Fleetwood and Patricroft, Manchester, in December. When the London Midland region had no further use for it as services had been taken over by diesel multiple-units, in June 1961 it was sent to the Southern Region, Brighton, where it was used before being despatched to Barnstaple in March 1963 and then transferred to Yeovil in September 1964. In June 1965 it was sent to Templecombe to work on the Somerset & Dorset from where it was withdrawn in March 1966 when that line closed. In June 1966 it was sold to Messrs Cohen and broken up at Morriston. During daylight hours the Southern Region used white discs rather than lamps. (Revd Alan Newman)

8 Standard Gauge Lines: The Midland Railway

THE EXPANSIONIST Midland Railway shrewdly leased the Bristol & Gloucester Railway in 1845 and sought an extension to Bath. The double-tracked line from Mangotsfield opened on 4 August 1869 and offered a faster and more direct route from Bath to the North, as well as an alternative route to Bristol. When the Somerset & Dorset Railway was opened from Bath to Bournemouth in 1874 it made what had hitherto been a branch line into a through route.

The Midland entered Somerset when it crossed the Avon south of Bitton station. There were no less than six graceful latticework bridges in five miles of route. With the planned introduction of heavier locomotives in the 1930s, five of those bridges were replaced by others of the box girder pattern, but replacing the bridge outside Bath station would have disturbed traffic to a greater extent than was acceptable, so that bridge was strengthened at every joint by welding. The bridge still exists today by Messrs Sainsbury's supermarket.

As the goods depot at Bath was south of the Avon and passenger facilities to the north, the road distance between the two was a mile. To obviate that problem the Midland constructed a road bridge. It was only wide enough for a single carriageway and by 1903 needed replacement. The new Midland Bridge was opened on 12 December 1905 and the redundant earlier bridge was bought by the city council and moved downstream to form the Destructor Bridge that stands today.

Passenger services on the line were withdrawn on 7 March 1966 and rail travellers going north, in addition to being denied a through service, had to travel to Bristol and change there. They were also charged a higher fare because of the greater distance travelled. Goods trains continued to run to Bath gas works, which received 3200 tons of coal weekly. With the introduction of North Sea gas and the consequent closure of Bath gas works in May 1971 the branch

closed on 28 May 1971 and the track lifted in the following year. From the outskirts of Bath westwards the formation was turned into a walkway and cycle track in 1979, the first major undertaking of its kind in Britain. The Bristol Suburban Railway, now the Avon Valley Railway, re-opened Bitton station in 1972, laid a length of track and is gradually extending its line towards Bath where it hopes to establish a terminus at Newbridge.

The small Kelston station was most unusual in that it had no goods sidings and no vehicle access. Kelston village was ¾ mile distant across fields and the station was actually nearer Saltford, which could be reached by a footpath beside the railway over the river. Kelston station was busy on the day of Saltford regatta, and when a race meeting was held on Lansdown passengers walked 2½ miles to the course, climbing 700ft. On those occasions railway police were in evidence as some bookies and punters tried to avoid paying fares. Most regular passengers using Kelston were fishermen. The last train called on 31 December 1948.

Weston station was of the typical Midland Railway twin-pavilion style. Tickets to the station were marked 'M & B' for Mangotsfield & Bath, to

Diesel-hydraulic D1045 *Western Viscount* heads a train of empty coal wagons west of Station Road level crossing, Bath, 28 May 1969. (Revd Alan Newman)

The approach to Bath Green Park station from the footplate, 1963. Centre left is a water column with a gas lamp to its left, while behind the lamp is the bonded store where spirits were kept. The original lattice bridges can be seen. (W F Grainger)

differentiate them from those to Weston super Mare. The opening of Bath Electric Tramways on 2 January 1904 seriously reduced the number of passengers using the station as trams provided a more frequent and cheaper service to the city. Only about a dozen people used the station daily prior to its closure on 21 September 1953.

The large goods depot at Bath was built on Sydenham Field, where W G Grace, then 15 years old, first played for the All-England Eleven against the Eighteen of Lansdown. There were two locomotive sheds at Bath: a stone-built one for Midland engines and a much larger one of timber construction for Somerset & Dorset engines. Fifty-one engines were allocated in 1950. Beside the shed a line ran down to the river. The Midland Railway operated a fleet of at least five boats at Bath, the waterway carrying traffic to Bradford on Avon and Trowbridge. The Midland's barge service at Bath ceased on 31 May 1912.

The splendid Georgian facade to the Midland station at Bath and its 66-ft span train shed is a Grade II listed building. Not many Bathonians were aware that the station had spacious cellars in which spirits were kept until closed in 1967.

9 Standard Gauge Lines: The Somerset & Dorset Railway

THE SOMERSET & Dorset had a highly complicated history. Basically, it consisted of two lines: the Somerset Central Railway and the Dorset Central Railway, which combined to offer a through route from the Bristol Channel to the English Channel. It constructed an extension over the Mendips to Bath, but its cost ruined the company. The Somerset & Dorset was purchased by the Midland Railway and the London & South Western Railway, so the line became the Somerset & Dorset Joint Railway.

In 1851 Glastonbury businessmen wanted a railway to carry their goods to the sea at Highbridge. The Bristol & Exeter Railway, owner of the Glastonbury Navigation and Canal, offered the canal in exchange for £8000-worth of shares. The broad gauge Somerset Central was built chiefly along the canal bank. Where soft ground was encountered, floating frames were provided to give a base for the track. It was one of the cheapest lines in England to construct, the total cost, including stations, surveying and Parliamentary expenses, worked out at £6560 per mile.

On 17 August 1854 the broad gauge line was ceremonially opened between Highbridge and Glastonbury and was worked by the Bristol & Exeter. On 3 May 1858 the extension to Burnham on Sea was opened, and beyond the station a 900-ft line ran down to a pier where vessels could land passengers from Cardiff at any state of the tide. Highbridge was the Somerset and Dorset's commercial port. The S&D had its own vessels until 1934, latterly only a cargo fleet.

The Somerset Central Railway built a mixed-gauge extension from Glastonbury to the standard gauge Dorset Central Railway at Bruton (later named 'Cole') and was opened on 3 February 1862. On 7 August 1862 the two companies combined to form the Somerset & Dorset Railway (S&D) and decided to abolish the broad gauge.

The Dorset Central Railway reached Bruton from Templecombe on 3 February 1862, the same date as the Somerset Central Railway reached it from Glastonbury. The through route between Cardiff and Cherbourg failed to prove the expected money-spinner and the S&D searched for another through route, since through routes paid better dividends than mere branch lines.

Women cleaners at Bath during World War I standing on S&D No 71 in blue livery. (Author's collection)

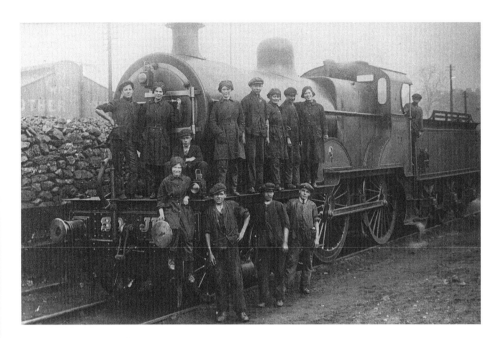

The challenging idea was adopted of extending from Evercreech over the Mendips to Bath, to link with the Midland Railway. In addition to creating a through route, quarries and collieries (500,000 tons mined in 1870) would be tapped *en route*. That extension was opened on 20 July 1874, and from that date the Bath to Bournemouth section became the main line, Burnham to Evercreech being relegated to secondary status. Although the extension brought an immediate increase in traffic, the company was financially exhausted and no money was left for sidings or even a proper supply of rolling stock. The S&D was faced with the choice of either going into receivership or being taken over by another company. The GWR was approached and in turn the GWR contacted its ally, the Bristol & Exeter. The latter showed little enthusiasm, and within two years it was to amalgamate with the GWR. Three months after the GWR had contacted the Bristol & Exeter, the London & South Western was brought into the negotiations to take over the S&D south of Templecombe. The South Western directors immediately approached the Midland Railway and sent an offer the same evening to the S&D, securing the line on a 99-year lease.

The line flourished under joint ownership – for instance, exchange traffic between the S&D and South Western at Templecombe was so great that in the early 1900s up to ten S&D goods trains left Templecombe between 10.00pm and 5.00am, while 21 goods trains ran from Bath plus five coal and stone trains from Radstock, Binegar or Winsor Hill. In 1910 203,571 wagons (a daily average of about 650) were exchanged at Templecombe. It was just as well that the precaution had been taken of doubling most of the line in Somerset.

Declining traffic caused all services to be withdrawn from the Wells branch on 29 October 1951; the Edington Junction to Bridgwater branch closed to passengers on 1 December 1952 and to goods on 1 October 1954, while Highbridge to Burnham closed to passengers on 29 October 1951 except for excursion traffic which continued until 8 September 1962. All through trains on the main line including the prestigious 'Pines Express' were withdrawn on 10 September 1962, all the S&D closing to passenger traffic and most of it to freight on 7 March 1966.

The S&D had running powers to the Midland station at Bath but the S&D itself began at Bath Junction. Most goods trains were banked at the rear up the two miles of 1 in 50 to Combe Down Tunnel, passing through Devonshire Tunnel (447 yd), named after a row of houses, Devonshire Buildings, above the tunnel. When the tunnel was cut it interfered with the wells of nearby residents and they had to be given an alternative supply. The railway piped water from

View from the brake van of the 11.00am Bath to Evercreech Junction goods train as it passes Writhlington signal box, 5 September 1960. A raft of empty wagons waits in the siding, left, ready to be shunted to the colliery. (Author)

Ex-S&D Sentinel vertical-boilered shunting engine No 47191 at Radstock 26 February 1953. (Revd Alan Newman)

the tunnel down to Bath for locomotive use. Combe Down Tunnel, 1 mile 69 yd long, was the longest single bore tunnel in Britain without a ventilating shaft. It was cut in the surprisingly short time of 15 months.

Midford station was built on the side of a cliff and its surrounds were so steep that its two goods yards had to be constructed some distance away. Beyond Midford the line became double track to Templecombe.

The line was very sinuous between Midford and Radstock and broadly followed the Radstock Tramway, built by the Somerset Coal Canal. Wellow station experienced good use until closure, because of a poor bus service. Shoscombe & Single Hill Halt opened on 23 September 1929 was constructed from concrete parts supplied by the Southern Railway's concrete depot at Exmouth Junction.

The S&D served several collieries in the Radstock area. Specially low shunting engines were required to pass below a bridge only 10ft 5in in height and between 1929 and 1961 Sentinel geared vertical boiler locomotives were used, similar to those used on the Whatley Quarry line. There was a stone-built engine shed at Radstock for housing those shunters and also the banking engines necessary for assisting goods trains up the 7½ miles of mainly 1 in 50 to the summit of the Mendips at Masbury, 811ft above sea level. Radstock engines burnt local coal but to prevent it from becoming treacle-like and blocking the access of air through the fire bars, plenty of limestone had to be placed in the fireboxes.

Midsomer Norton station, once famed for its greenhouse and most attractive gardens, has been re-opened together with a short length of line and is to be extended as funds permit. Chilcompton station was used by Downside School,

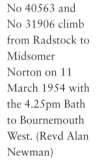

No 40563 and No 31906 climb from Radstock to Midsomer Norton on 11 March 1954 with the 4.25pm Bath to Bournemouth West. (Revd Alan Newman)

with specials at the beginning and end of each term. From Binegar station a 2ft 6in gauge line ran to Oakhill Brewery. It carried 'Invalid Stout'. Before World War I the brewery's output was 2000 to 2500 barrels weekly, but traffic declined in post-war years when drink fell from favour. The line had closed by 1921 when the track was lifted. It was worked by two 0-4-0 saddle tanks engines, *Mendip* and *Oakhill*.

From Masbury Summit the line descended at 1 to 50 to Evercreech Junction. Above the bay window of Masbury station was a carving of Maesbury Castle, a medieval design because the sculptor was evidently unaware that the castle dated back to the Iron Age. At one time the station master was an ardent Wesleyan and on Sundays held services in the waiting room, using a harmonium to accompany the singing. Hamwood Viaduct, 72yd long, spanned a wooded ravine and beyond were the twin Winsor Hill tunnels. The down tunnel was the original, curved and 239yd long. During its construction four navvies were killed and were buried in Shepton Mallet cemetery under a monument made from rock that caused their death. The newer up tunnel is straight, lined throughout and only 126yd long.

(Left) Ex-S&D heavy goods locomotive No 53809 about to leave Norton Hill Colliery with a down mineral train 15 April 1955 (Revd Alan Newman)

(Top right) No 58072 at Midsomer Norton with the 6.05pm Bath to Binegar, 25 April 1955. This engine was built for use in London tunnels and could condense the steam to ameliorate, to some extent, unpleasant conditions in tunnels. (Revd Alan Newman)

No 47557 trapped in a snowdrift near Winsor Hill Tunnel, 5 January 1963. A rescue train is on the far left. To avoid the boiler becoming dry the fire has been extinguished. (John Stamp)

Ex-S&D No 43201
at Evercreech
Junction on 26 April
1954 with a train to
Highbridge. (Revd
Alan Newman)

No 41206 on the
turntable at
Templecombe, 28
February 1966.
Notice the permanent
ladder to the engine
shed roof. (Revd Alan
Newman)

Two arches of the 118yd Bath Road Viaduct at Shepton Mallet collapsed in 1946 and two of the remaining four had to be demolished. The rebuilding was done in mass concrete and the piers faced with brindle brick. The most impressive Charlton Viaduct, 308yd long, has 27 arches. Beyond Shepton Mallet station the line passed below the East Somerset Railway and crossed the 121yd Prestleigh Viaduct. Evercreech Junction was an important locomotive point where pilot engines for heavy passengers trains were coupled or detached and train engines stopped to replenish their water tanks.

The S&D crossed the Wilts, Somerset & Weymouth Railway by a 5-arch viaduct north of Cole, whose station was built in typical Dorset Central Railway style with high gables, tall chimneys and a hipped roof to the waiting room and booking office. Templecombe was the junction with the South Western and most S&D passenger trains called at the South Western station, requiring a time-wasting procedure of either reversing in or out. South of Templecombe the line entered Dorset.

The Highbridge Branch

Just over a mile beyond Evercreech Junction the single-track Highbridge line descended the 4-mile Pylle Bank at 1 in 100. Pylle had what was probably a unique goods shed with one end containing the station house. Between 7 December 1891 and 8 December 1929 it had a second platform enabling two passenger trains to cross. West Pennard, in similar style to Pylle, retained its second platform until 26 April 1964.

Glastonbury was a busy intermediate station with two platforms for the main line, the outer face of the down being used by branch trains to Wells. The wooden station buildings had a bookstall and refreshment room. The S&D engineer's workshops were at Glastonbury. The original platform at Ashcott was of timber but was replaced in the 1920s by a concrete structure from Exmouth Junction Works. The platform had no shelter but a booking office and waiting room were adjacent to the level crossing. Peat was despatched from the small goods yard. Beyond were peat workings and on a misty morning 19 August 1949, 0-6-0 No 3260 struck a narrow-gauge engine and plunged into the South Drain.

Floods at Glastonbury & Street station c 1900. (Author's collection)

The two-platform station at Shapwick was a mile from Westhay and twice that distance from Shapwick. The original platforms for the passing loop were formed by timber walls with earth banked up behind, but in the 1930s were replaced by concrete components. The building on the up platform – the southernmost – caught fire on 25 September 1900 and was replaced by a timber office building. Peat traffic was important. Edington Junction had two main-line platforms and a bay for Bridgwater trains. Bason Bridge station opened in July 1856, a couple of years after the line opened. It had buildings of timber construction. A large milk factory opened in 1909 adjacent to the station and milk traffic continued until 2 October 1972.

On the south side of the line just before Highbridge station were buildings that until 1930 housed the S&D locomotive, carriage and wagon works. Its closure was a tragedy for the town as 300 men lost their jobs and there was no comparable industry in the area to absorb them. During World War II there was a United States' Ordnance Depot with 7 miles of sidings opposite the former works. United States' troops manned London, Midland & Scottish Railway engines and provided their own guards and shunters from Highbridge Wharf to

No 58086 at Highbridge shed, 29 August 1956. Notice the rack of fire irons. The shed closed on 11 May 1959. (Author)

A winch steam crane at Highbridge Wharf *c* 1900. (Author's collection)

the camp. Beyond the S&D station, with five platforms, the GWR was crossed on the level. Highbridge Wharf was busy until its latter years, closing in 1949. Burnham had two platforms, the ordinary one covered and the excursion open. At times it was very busy, dealing with up to 10,000 excursionists daily. In earlier days the line extended down a gradient of 1 in 23 to the pier, and latterly those rails were used by the launching cradle of the lifeboat.

(Left) The S&D War Memorial at Highbridge Works on 11 November in the 1920s. (Author's collection)

(Right) Rails in the jetty at Burnham on Sea, 29 August 1956. Originally these carried passenger coaches down to the cross-channel ferry, but in later years they were used for trans-porting the lifeboat on a wheeled cradle. (Author)

The locomotive erecting and fitting shop, Highbridge, pre-1895. (Author's collection)

Glastonbury to Wells

The S&D opened its branch from Glastonbury to Wells on 3 March 1859. Two large signs on Wells Town Hall looked rather curious in juxtaposition: 'The earth is the Lord's and all that therein is' and 'Cheer boys, cheer, there's wealth for honest labour'. Originally there was no intermediate station, but one was opened in December 1861 at Polsham. A red-brick booking office block was erected on the platform in 1894 and a station master's house in the 1920s. The station was reduced to halt status in July 1938.

Until 2 December 1878 a train for Wells diverged from the Evercreech line 1 mile east of Glastonbury, but on that date the signal box closed and a parallel line from Glastonbury was brought into use. Just before reaching Wells station the engine shed was passed. The two-road shed was demolished in 1956, having been closed temporarily in April 1935 because the original rails were in very poor condition and needed to be replaced. From then on the GWR shed at Wells provided temporary hospitality for S&D engines. The S&D opened a splendid pumping station in 1861 where a wheel lifted water for locomotive use. The S&D water tank at Wells had a private pipe connection to supply a farm whose water supply had been cut off by the diversion of a stream when the branch was built. The crossing keepers at Coxley and Polsham were supplied with water from Wells in 8-gallon cans, trains stopping regularly to drop them off. The single-road S&D stone station at Priory Road in Wells was quite a grand affair, befitting a cathedral city, and had a timber train shed.

The name plate of 'West Country' class No 34092 *City of Wells* after it had been renamed from simply *Wells*. (Dr A J G Dickens)

The largest engine to travel on the branch was the Southern Railway 'West Country' class Pacific No 34092 *City of Wells*, built at Brighton in 1949. It travelled along the line for its naming ceremony. That engine is now preserved by the Keighley & Worth Valley Railway. The Wells branch closed entirely on 29 October 1951.

Edington Junction to Bridgwater

The Bridgwater Railway opened on 21 July 1890, a typically wet summer day; it rained so heavily that the civic reception had to be abandoned. The nominally independent railway, although virtually part of the S&D and worked by that company, was nominally worked by the South Western. Perhaps surprisingly, the Bridgwater Railway paid a dividend of 4½% for many years and remained independent until absorbed by the South Western on 31 December 1922. Because of declining traffic the single-coach passenger service was withdrawn on 1 December 1952 and the branch goods service on 1 October 1954. However, goods traffic continued to use Bridgwater North station, gaining access over former GWR lines, until the yard was closed on 7 July 1962.

Branch passenger trains left the outer face of the island platform at Edington

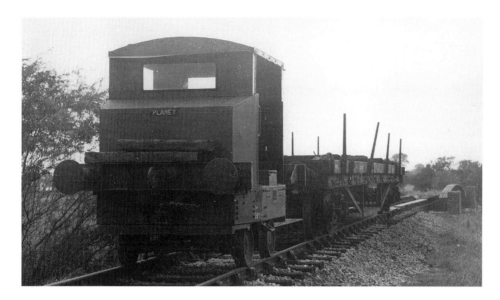

'Planet' locomotive track-lifting on the Bridgwater branch just west of Edington Burtle, 29 August 1956. (Author)

Cossington station and former station master's house, 29 August 1956. Nearest to the photographer is a ground frame hut (a mini signal box). Point rodding that has tunnelled beneath the platform can be seen to the left of the track. (Author)

Junction and rose on a gradient of 1 in 72 to a summit on the Poldens at Cossington. Dominating the stone-built single-story station office building was the station master's house. The line descended at 1 in 72 to Bawdrip Halt, opened on 7 July 1923 following the receipt of a petition with 182 signatures. The halt's components came from the Exmouth Junction concrete depot. With 200 passengers using it weekly, a request for a shelter was submitted in 1924 and a concrete shelter appeared.

Bridgwater North station had a red brick building set at right angles to the buffers. The two 300-ft platforms were sheltered by a canopy 200ft in length. The single road brick-built engine shed was extended in 1898 to accommodate two locomotives. No engines were stabled there overnight after 1922 and in 1928 the building was leased to the Co-operative Society as a store. The turntable remained in use.

Until its closure in 1942, a line about ½ mile in length led from the station past the cement works to a wharf on the River Parrett. Up to 1920 a rail-mounted travelling steam crane, built by Thomas Smith of Leeds, was used at the wharf.

10 **Minor Lines**

West Somerset Mineral Railway

In the middle of the 19th century iron ore was mined at Gupworthy and Raleigh's Cross on the Brendon Hills, but the only means of transporting it to ships at Watchet was by horse and cart. In 1855 an Act was obtained for the Brendon Hill Ore Company to construct a line 13¼ miles in length, including an impressive incline ¾- mile long on a gradient of 1 in 4, known as Combe Row Incline. It literally was an independent railway and had no rail link with any other line.

Its first locomotive arrived in 1856, unfortunately killing a horse on the way. Apparently the cart carrying the engine overran one of the animals drawing it. That engine was dogged with misfortune as in the following year it was damaged when the fireman carelessly lit the fire under an empty boiler. A second locomotive was bought and the first was returned to its makers for repair.

Soon after opening in April 1857 disaster struck. On 21 August 1857 the engine left Roadwater drawing a truckload of men to collect their pay. At Washford the driver was instructed to wait for a coal train from Watchet. However, the railway's assistant engineer, riding on the footplate, was in a hurry to catch the evening post. He countermanded the order and the two trains collided, killing three men, while escaping steam scalded several others. Both engines were unusable and another had to be bought.

The incline was opened in the following year, but the section proved very expensive. It cost over £82,000, yet the estimate for the whole railway had been only £65,000. The first passenger train ran on 7 August 1860 carrying about 800 people to a temperance meeting. As the railway had no coaches at the time they were carried in open tucks. A regular passenger service started on 4 September 1865.

A West Somerset Mineral Railway Company proxy form for the meeting on 25 September 1918.

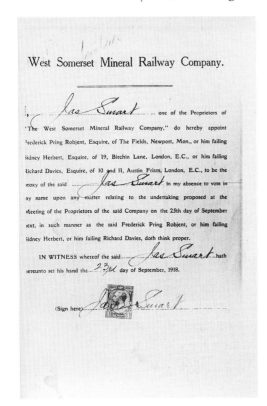

144

There was no official passenger service up the incline but people were allowed to travel free at their own risk. The 13,297 passengers carried by the West Somerset Mineral Railway in 1866 grew to 19,268 in 1872 and the railway was able to claim that no fare-paying passenger was ever killed.

It was inevitable that some sort of mishap would occur on the incline. In November 1882 as two wagons were being coupled to an engine at the top their weight started pulling the locomotive down the gradient. All the vehicles were derailed by catch points and bounced down the incline over the sleepers. Half way down the leading truck slewed across the line, halting further progress.

With the closure of all the mines by June 1883, railway traffic became lighter. There were now no loaded descending iron ore wagons to draw trucks up the incline and a stationary steam engine had to be installed. As the mine branches were no longer required they were lifted and the materials used for repairing the main line, which had become rather unsafe.

The Board of Trade required continuous brakes to be fitted on passenger coaches. As it happened, the West Somerset Mineral Railway's second-hand coaches were already fitted with vacuum brakes when purchased, but were of little use as the engine was not equipped to work them. Eventually, in 1894 *Pontypool* was fitted with a vacuum brake. Traffic dwindled to such an extent that the line was closed on 7 November 1898. In order that the rolling stock could be removed to their owners at Ebbw Vale the GWR slewed its track near the vicinity of the later Kentsford Loop. The train consisted of three GWR engines to provide haulage power, the Mineral Railway's *Pontypool*, two coaches, a GWR mess coach and approximately 50 wagons. At the GWR's Watchet station the train was divided into three more manageable portions. On 4 June 1899 the line was again temporarily slewed to allow the Mineral railway engine *Newport* to be removed. As the GWR would not permit it to travel on

The dramatic rope-worked Combe Row incline *c* 1897. (Author's collection)

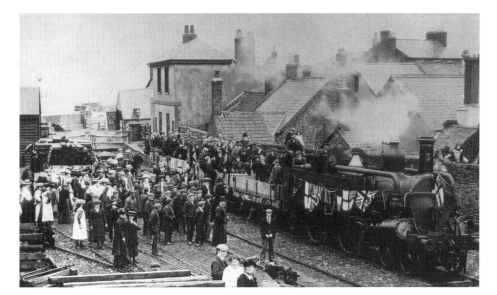

Watchet on 4 July 1907. The wagons contain Watchet Council members and the town band on the inaugural train when the line was re-opened. The engine came from the Metropolitan Railway. (Bert Hole)

its own wheels, on reaching the GWR station at Watchet it was craned on to a 'Crocodile' wagon.

In 1907 the Somerset Mineral Syndicate Limited was formed to re-open the mines. The railway was repaired and once more the line was slewed at Kentsford. A slump occurred in the steel trade in the following year so a temporary connection was put in to remove an engine and 21 wagons.

On 17 December 1911 the West Somerset Mineral Railway was leased by an Australian company, A R Angus Limited, which used the line from Watchet to Williton to demonstrate its patent automatic train control. Two ex-GWR 2-4-0 tender engines were purchased and a connection made yet again at Kentsford.

That train control system used no signals, but an electric ramp between the rails showed a disc to the driver or blew a whistle; and if the warning was ignored the regulator on the locomotive was closed and the brakes automatically applied. The public demonstrations were highly dramatic. Locomotives were started from either end as for a head-on collision and the drivers and firemen leaped off. The whistles automatically blew and the engines came to rest 200yd apart. On one occasion a spectator was no less than the Tsar of Russia's uncle. The exhibitions continued until the end of 1914 when the equipment was removed. The line was dismantled in 1917-18. In September 1918 the line was resuscitated when the Timber Supply Department of the Board of Trade asked permission to lay a narrow gauge light railway from the government saw mills at Washford to the harbour at Watchet. Mules were used to haul the wagons, but the line was lifted early in 1920, bringing the history of this fascinating railway to a close.

Some of the remaining buildings of the railway have been declared Scheduled Ancient Monuments by English Heritage. It is hoped to secure funds to improve

Ex-GWR No 213 used for the Angus tests. (Author's collection)

The former West Somerset Mineral Railway goods shed at Watchet, in use as a garage, 30 June 1967. Car parking is 1s. (Author)

access to Combe Row Incline. Watchet Town Council has allocated £4000 towards the creation of a model of the incline to be housed at the town's museum. At Watchet the two-story station master's house is still extant, as is the former goods shed. Washford station was a square stone building with a canopy sheltering the platform. Roadwater was of a similar design and still survives as part of a private bungalow, Combe Row was also similar and the former station master's house still stands at the foot of the incline. Various traces of the line can still be seen at the top of the incline.

Weston, Clevedon & Portishead Light Railway

At Portishead the GWR linked with the Weston, Clevedon & Portishead Light Railway, managed for many years by Colonel H F Stephens. It was one of those delightful lines where passengers could pick blackberries from a moving train and it was not unknown for the driver, fireman and guard of the first morning train to stop *en route* to pick mushrooms to be fried with bacon on a shovel after arrival at Weston super Mare.

Initially, four miles of line were built from Weston super Mare, but financial difficulties, coupled with the contractor's failure, brought work to a halt. After two more contractors had made efforts and given up, the line was eventually completed to Clevedon by the company itself. Colonel Sir F Marindin, inspecting the line of behalf of the Board of Trade, was far from impressed. In places the line had been laid for so many years that the sleepers had rotted, there were gaps in the hedges and level-crossing gates were missing. Shortly after the inspection J F R Daniel, the managing director, wrote to Marindin saying that about two dozen level-crossing gates had been found at Clevedon and hitherto no one knew what they were for; they were now being

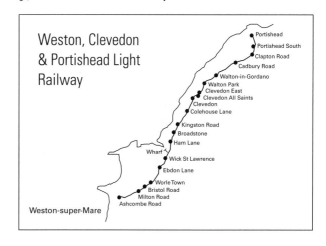

Weston, Clevedon & Portishead Light Railway

Portishead
Portishead South
Clapton Road
Cadbury Road
Walton-in-Gordano
Walton Park
Clevedon East
Clevedon All Saints
Clevedon
Colehouse Lane
Kingston Road
Broadstone
Ham Lane
Wharf
Wick St Lawrence
Ebdon Lane
Worle Town
Bristol Road
Milton Road
Ashcombe Road
Weston-super-Mare

De-railed *Weston*
(before naming) and
coach near Kingston
Road, 5 June 1899.
The fence has been
laid flat. *Portishead*,
left, has come to the
rescue. (G Rushton
collection)

A selection of
Weston, Clevedon &
Portishead Light
Railway tickets.

The engine later
named *Hesperus* at
Weston super Mare
with an American-
type coach.
(Author's collection)

erected. Marindin was amazed that at the time of his inspection not even one locomotive was on order.

Weston super Mare Urban District Council justifiably complained that the rails of the street section in Ashcombe Road, Milton Road, Gerard Road and the Boulevard protruded dangerously, so the railway company removed them. The line between Clevedon and Weston was eventually opened on 1 December 1897. A horse bus linked Portishead with Clevedon and connected with trains. Later the horse bus was replaced by an early motor bus built by Richard Stephens of Clevedon.

In 1904 work started on completing the line through to Portishead and it was opened on 7 August 1907. The cost of the extension placed the company in financial straits and in 1909 a receiver was appointed. In the following year a Light Railway Order was obtained for linking the railway with the Locking Road tramway of Weston super Mare & District Electric Supply Company, but the project failed to reach fruition. Had it done so, the light railway's fortunes might have improved as it would have had access to the sea, instead of leaving its passengers high and dry ¾ mile from the beach. In 1940 the sole creditor of the railway, the Excess Insurance Company, decided to cut its losses and withdraw. A Court Order was made and the line closed after the last train ran on 18 May. The GWR took over the line temporarily for storing loaded coal wagons that had become an embarrassment following the cessation of coal exports after the evacuation of Dunkirk. The track was lifted in 1942.

No less than 16 steam locomotives worked on the line at one time or another, though most were bought second- or even third-hand. By contrast the first coaches were new and originally destined for a South American railway. The bodies were entirely of mahogany and were made in sections held together by brass screws for easy 'knocking down' for shipping. They were unusual for this country, and having open verandahs at each end looked like something from

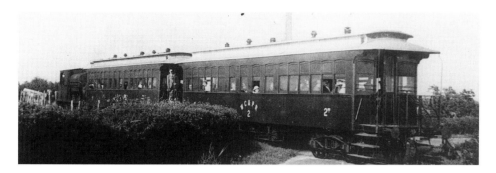

Ebdon Lane station, September 1936. Most WC&PLR stations had no platforms so, in lieu, trains stopped with the steps in the middle of the road. (Author's collection)

a Wild West film. They were ideal for enabling the conductor to pass from one coach to the next collecting fares. With the opening of the Portishead section some second-hand coaches that had been used on the London underground system were bought from the Metropolitan Railway.

Soon after World War I the Weston, Clevedon & Portishead made early essays with petrol-engined railway vehicles. A railcar seating 30 passengers was bought, its running and maintenance costs being a mere 6d a mile. During busy periods a 24-seater trailer was coupled on. Spare cans of petrol, often with caps missing, were carried in the railcar and as smoking was not prohibited it was most fortunate that no accident occurred. Pleased with the success of the railcar, the company purchased a Fordson tractor fitted with railway wheels and used it as a shunter. While being towed from Wick St Lawrence to Clevedon at the rear of a train it jumped the rails and was damaged beyond repair before the train could be halted.

WC&PLR conductor Bill Cullen, c 1909. (Author's collection)

Wick St Lawrence was the junction of a short branch to a wharf on the River Yeo. The company made it sound grandiose and displayed notices announcing: 'Seaborne traffic can now be dealt with at Wick St Lawrence'. Weight restrictions only permitted three wagons on the wharf at a time and they were either dragged off by steel hawser attached to the tractor or eased off with a pinch bar. Most, if not all, the trade was with South Wales and supplies of coal for the locomotives and Clevedon gas works came via that route. The railway owned several sailing barges.

One novel innovation in the 1930s was the installation of traffic lights to protect ungated level crossings as an Act of Parliament had allowed the gates to be removed. A green light was normally favourable to the road, but an approaching train operated a track treadle and the lights changed to red. Enterprising boys were also able to make use of the treadle.

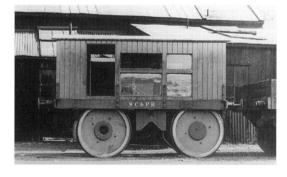

As the Weston, Clevedon & Portishead always had financial problems all its stations had single platforms, even the termini and its headquarters at Clevedon – which made it interesting when two passenger trains had to cross. The inconvenient position of the station at Weston has already been mentioned. The original timber platform, only 10in above the ground level, was replaced in 1919

The Muir-Hill internal-combustion engine shunter at Clevedon. Brakes are only on one set of wheels. (Author's collection)

by a standard height timber platform and waiting shelter of the same material.
The separate station offices of timber had a semi-circular corrugated-iron roof.
Milton Road Halt, like all halts on the line, had no platform and was just a
gravelled area with waiting shelter. That particular hut was designed by Colonel
Stephens when travelling in the brake van with Guard Carey. Its asbestos walls
were kicked in by children so they were covered with corrugated iron. Bristol
Road Halt had no platform or shelter and as at most of the halts the driver drew
up carefully so that two of the coach verandahs were in the centre of the road.

Worle Town seems a curious name today but in the 19th century it was the
market town for Weston. Its timber building was a combined booking office
and shelter. Ebdon Lane Halt had a small timber shelter not much larger than a
sentry box. Wick St Lawrence had a midway crossing loop and like Worle the
timber building was a combined booking office and waiting shelter. The village
was completely dependent on the railway for passengers and goods transport.
The manager of a Weston bank lived at Wick and if he was not at the station in
the morning a member of the train crew called at his home, other passengers
being kept waiting while he shaved and making children late for school. On
Friday mornings villagers took chickens to the butcher and no extra fare was
charged. Bundles of newspapers from Weston were thrown out by the guard at
Wick if the train did not stop and villagers collected from the shed.

Beyond the siding to the wharf, the Yeo was crossed by a 7-span bridge
240ft in length. The two piers nearest Clevedon sank soon after erection, the dip

Broadstone station – just a hut and timetable. The cattle grid on the far side of the lane prevents animals from wandering along the track. Beyond the cattle grid is a bridge over a rhyne. (Author's collection)

needing timber supports. Check rails inside both running rails guarded against derailment. Mud Lane crossing had a sleeper-built milk platform. Ham Lane Halt had a wooden shelter and its milk platform had been adapted from the base of an old wagon. Locally-cut peat was loaded at the siding. Broadstone Halt had what was really a one-person shelter and that at Kingston Road was not much larger. Colehouse Lane Halt had a different pattern and was long and narrow.

Clevedon originally had a 10in high platform but one of standard height with waiting shelter was erected in 1919. The office building, of similar design to that at Weston super Mare, was situated on the opposite side of the line, as were the locomotive and carriage sheds. Beyond the station, Lower Queen's Road level crossing had three large gates, lever-worked from a cabin. As the largest gate closed unseen from the cabin a warning bell rang before it was moved. As the gates did not close off the railway completely, the gatekeeper walked across in front of the train carrying two flags: a red to give warning and a green to call on the train. A ¼-mile siding led to Clevedon gas works, most of its coal coming from Wick Wharf. The gas works tar wagon carried the product to Butler's Chemical Works, Bristol, and periodically ammonical liquor from the gas works was sprayed all over the light railway's tracks to kill weeds. A nearby siding served the Munition Box Works that after World War I became Shopland's saw mills.

Clevedon East Halt had a waiting shelter and siding to Weech's Joinery Works, the firm receiving consignments of 20 or more wagons. Beyond, the line climbed at 1 in 116 through the picturesque Swiss Valley. All Saints' Halt had no shelter. The level crossing had two sets of gates that, like those at Clevedon, were operated by levers rather than a wheel; difficulties could be experienced in a strong wind. The gates were opened by the blacksmith as a part-time job. Beyond the crossing the line steepened to 1 in 68 up and the gradient could cause a serious problem for a well-worn locomotive hauling a heavy train.

Walton Park Halt, just beyond the summit, had an attractive rustic-style timber shelter very much like a garden summer-house. A siding led to Conygar Quarry. Walton-in-Gordano Halt had a roomy waiting shelter as did Cadbury Road Halt. Beyond that were Black Rock Quarry Sidings holding 90 wagons. Those sidings were served by a narrow-gauge railway. Most of the Clevedon to Portishead passenger trains called at the sidings and collected up to about 10

The transfer siding at Black Rock Quarry, 1921. The nearest standard gauge wagon is owned by the Lancashire & Yorkshire Railway, with GWR and MR wagons beyond. On the loading bank is one of the quarry's 2ft gauge loco-motives built by Hudswell, Clarke & Co Ltd, Leeds, in 1919. (Author's collection)

loaded wagons, a total of 40 or upwards being removed in a busy day. In 1934 an average of 75 wagons daily left Conygar and Black Rock quarries bringing an income of £3050, compared with £750 for passengers.

Clapton Road Halt had no shelter but Portishead South had a fair-sized timber one. Coal arrived at the siding for a merchant and bricks and tiles were despatched. Portishead station had a rustic-style building combining offices and waiting shelter and formed the line's most attractive station. Messrs Mustad's nail works had its own siding for receiving consignments of raw material and the despatch of the finished product. Beyond the station, traffic was exchanged with the GWR.

The rural surroundings of the WC&PLR's Portishead station on 7 August 1907, the opening day. Later, Mustad's nail factory was built in the field on the left. The locomotive is running round its train. (M J Tozer collection)

11 Significant Accidents

NORTON FITZWARREN proved an unlucky station for railway accidents and was the site of two major tragedies. The broad gauge was inherently safe and what would have been a disaster on a standard gauge line proved only fatal to the footplate crew in the accident in 1890. The Bristol & Exeter in fact claimed that it never killed a passenger but its successor, the GWR, was not so lucky.

Around 12.30am on 11 November 1890 the 6.45pm ex-Bristol down goods was shunting the sidings at Norton. Although a standard gauge train headed by a standard gauge engine, it was assisted in front by a broad gauge locomotive. As only one engine was required for shunting operations the broad gauge engine was uncoupled and temporarily sent out of the way a short distance down the Barnstaple branch.

Shunting had been completed and the 9.55pm ex-Bristol fast down goods was almost due so the signalman sent the 6.45pm train over to the up line to allow the 9.55 to overtake. As he was then on the 'wrong' line, Driver Charles Noble changed his headlight from the normal green to a warning red one. When the 9.55 passed Noble changed it back to green in anticipation of the signalman giving him the 'All clear'.

Sadly that did not happen because the signalman had completely forgotten about the down goods standing on the up line and accepted a special Plymouth to Paddington train conveying passengers and mail from a South African liner. The special, only two coaches and a van, came hurtling towards Norton at 60mph, its driver having no warning of the obstruction as its lights were green and not red.

Despite the 60-mph impact the broad gauge locomotive and train remained upright but the goods train wreckage piled 30ft. The crew of the broad gauge engine were badly, but not fatally, injured but 10 of the 50 passengers were killed, a large proportion of them miners returning to the North of England from the South African gold mines.

The Norton
Fitzwarren accident
on 11 November
1890: the standard
gauge goods engine
is nearest the artist,
with broad gauge
passenger engine
beyond. (Author's
collection)

The Norton
Fitzwarren accident
on 11 November
1890: the standard
gauge goods engine
is nearest the artist,
with broad gauge
passenger engine
beyond. (Author's
collection)

To prevent a repetition of the accident a rule was adopted by all British railways that when a train halted at a signal the driver was to blow his whistle and if the signalman did not lower his 'board' after three minutes in clear weather, or immediately in fog or falling snow, he must send a fireman, guard or shunter to the signal box to inform the signalman of the train's presence and not leave until a collar had been placed over the relevant signal lever to prevent a conflicting movement being made. Additionally, that person was to sign the train register.

And what happened to the engines involved? As the end of the broad gauge was near, the broad gauge engine was scrapped but the standard gauge one was repaired and returned to service. She was sold to the Government in 1916 and was sent to Serbia to haul military trains for the Railway Operating Division. She never returned to England.

The second disaster at Norton Fitzwarren occurred almost exactly fifty years after the first. On 4 November 1940 the 9.50pm Paddington to Penzance sleeping car express called at Taunton. Usually, immediately after leaving the station the express was crossed to the down main line, but as the signalman had been advised that the 12.50am ex-Paddington newspaper train was running early and as it was not booked to call at Taunton, he correctly decided to let it run through on the main line and to send the express as far as Norton on the parallel relief line.

However, the express driver, not realising he was on the relief line, mistook the main line signals cleared for the newspaper train as his own. Not until the other engine drew alongside just before reaching Norton did he realise his error. He immediately closed the regulator and applied the brakes but there was no time to stop before his engine ran out of track at the end of the relief line.

The first six coaches derailed across all four tracks and of the 900 passengers 27 were killed. Serious though that was, it would have been far worse had the newspaper train been a few seconds later and crashed into the wreckage instead of running clear. It was an extremely close thing, for the lower panels of the last newspaper van were found to be marked by ballast flung up by the derailed express.

The Norton Fitzwarren area was the scene of yet another disaster on 6 July 1978. As the 21.30 Penzance to Paddington sleeper passed through Whiteball Tunnel, the sleeping car attendant for the rear coaches smelled burning. He checked his own coaches, lettered D and E, and also found smoke in C, third from the front. He returned to D and pulled the alarm signal. He tried to return to C to alert passengers but smoke coming back from Car B forced him back. As the train stopped he found the attendant for Cars B and C lying in the corridor of Car C and helped him out. Firemen with breathing apparatus were held back by the terrific heat and could not enter until the coach had been hosed down. Twelve passengers died.

What caused the fire? Two piles of linen bags, one of soiled linen from the previous night and the other bags of clean linen had been stacked in the leading vestibule of Car B against a switched-on electric heater. Although fire-retardant materials were used for constructing the sleeping cars, subsequent replacements were not to the same standard. Most of those who died had inhaled large amounts of cyanide and carbon monoxide; the air ventilator ducts actually helped to distribute the fumes.

There were other, fortunately less serious accidents in other parts of the county's network. As the original Somerset & Dorset Railway was single lined, trains passed each other at established stations. If a train was running late a decision had to be taken as to how long another would wait for it. Caleb Percy in his office at Glastonbury was responsible for crossing trains running out of course and was in contact with stations by means of a single needle telegraph.

Bank Holiday Monday, 7 August 1876, had been very busy with 17 extra trains. The 7.10pm Wimborne to Bath relief was drawn by a new, powerful engine and reached Radstock 15 minutes before Percy's calculations. Station master John Jarrett tried to contact Percy for instructions, was unable to reach him and, instead of holding the train until an answer was received, sent it on.

Between Radstock and Wellow a signal box called Foxcote and later Writhlington had been opened the previous year to work a colliery siding. It had no crossing loop but merely worked the siding and passed on trains. It had no communication with Glastonbury. Things were slack at Foxcote. Only the home signals were lit and both distant signals were unlit because they had run out of oil and it was the frugal practice of the S&D not to light them on moonlit nights. When the 7.10 arrived Signalman Dando held the train, checked that the line was clear to Wellow and sent it forward.

Unfortunately, matters were also slack at Wellow. Station master Sleep had been on duty from 5.00am until 6.30pm and he went off to quench his thirst at the Hope & Anchor in Midford. On such a busy day he should have remained at his post. In charge during his absence was 15-year-old telegraph clerk Arthur Hillard despite a rule which stipulated that a telegraph clerk was not allowed to signal 'Line clear' unless authorised by the station master.

A special train carrying spectators from the Saltford Regatta should have left Bath at 9.15pm, arrived at Radstock at 9.45 and returned to Bath before the Wimborne train arrived, but it had been seriously delayed and did not actually

No 6028 *King George VI* at Norton Fitzwarren on 4 November 1940. No 6028 was originally named *King Henry II* but with the accession of King George was renamed in January 1937. The cab side-window is blocked out by a steel sheet so that the fire did not infringe blackout regulations. (Author's collection)

leave Bath until 10.43. In due course it arrived at Wellow with Mr Sleep as a passenger from Midford. At 11.3pm it was sent on by Hillard, who claimed that he had received 'Line clear' from Foxcote.

There were now two trains approaching each other head-on between Wellow and Foxcote. Driver John Hamlin on the very late 9.15 from Bath saw the up train approaching and was able to place his engine in reverse before the two collided 247yd east of Foxcote. The first three coaches of the 9.15 were smashed, killing 10 adults, 2 children and the guard. None of the passengers on the other train were killed and its coaches were only slightly damaged. Mr Coombs of the Bell Hotel, Radstock, 'supplied a liberal quantity of spirits' to the wounded and his hotel, the Waldegrave Arms, Radstock, accommodated passengers unable to complete their journey. The corpses were taken to the barn of the adjacent Paglinch Farm and were laid out to be identified. Unfortunately they proved to be a magnet for the ghoulish and both the coroner and the local vicar told the crowd that they hoped that only the immediate relatives would view the bodies. Numerous articles belonging to the killed and injured were stolen from the wreckage.

Messrs Powell & Powell, auctioneers of Bath, for £46 provided coffins for the 11 adults and 2 children. They were conveyed to Paglinch Farm by special train. The S&D paid about £9000 in compensation and four children orphaned by the accident were offered employment, three eventually rising to become station masters and one a head-office inspector.

James Sleep was found guilty of manslaughter and sentenced to 12 months imprisonment without hard labour. Caleb Percy was dismissed with one month's salary in lieu of notice; station master Jarrett, like Sleep, was dismissed.

12 **An Overview**

WHAT HAVE railways done for Somerset? Before the coming of railways life in the county moved at a slow pace – even getting from one side of Somerset to the other was impossible in a day except on a very few stage-coach routes. For many, travel was unnecessary because they lived and worked within walking distance of their homes. Agriculture was mostly dairying, the climate favouring meadows, and butter and cheese stayed fresh long enough to travel to market. Oats were important as horse feed for coaching inns. The introduction of railways caused a dramatic change to the lives of some innkeepers and farmers; innkeepers on once busy roads lost their trade, and farmers had to change to growing other crops.

The railway station developed as a social centre with shops or stalls starting up nearby, assured of regular trade. The station master was a man of importance, ranking with the doctor, rector and school headmaster. A good station master made it his job to keep in touch with local developments, for he was responsible for bringing business to his railway. In the 19th century a town with a railway thrived, a town without a railway tended to become a backwater.

The railway offered a greater variety of employment than had been available in the district before its arrival. To progress through the railway ranks one needed to move, no longer staying in the same house or even in the same native village. Sometimes only a day's notice was given to report to another station.

The coming of the railway led to a greater use of coal for cooking and heating than hitherto unless home was near a pit or waterway or the sea, for transportation of coal was expensive and wood was the alternative fuel. A greater variety of building material could also be used, not just local stone or brick but different materials brought cheaply from a distance such as slates and tiles which rendered thatch out of date.

With cheap transport, industry could develop: a shoe or chocolate factory need no longer just supply the district but the whole country or even the whole world. The railway enabled the cottager's wife to travel to a larger market town where she could receive a better price for her butter, cheese and eggs, more than offsetting the cost of her ticket.

Railways affected diet. No longer did one have to rely on what was grown in one's garden or was grown locally. Food could be transported cheaply from or to other parts of the country. Cattle, rabbits and strawberries were sent from Somerset and early potatoes and tomatoes brought in, while such things as bananas could be imported and distributed.

Railways enabled people to gain a broader understanding by travel. The Great Exhibition of 1851 could be reached by cheap excursion from Somerset and that meant that many people visited the metropolis who would not otherwise have done so. Quite a few shops and firms paid the fare for their employees.

The Workmen's Early Morning Return enabled people to travel cheaply by rail as long as they reached their destination by 8.00am. That time limit was imposed to prevent white collar workers who were better paid and could afford a full price or season ticket from taking advantage of cheap fares.

Railways enabled seaside resorts to develop from fishing villages or select watering places only visited by the rich: Minehead, Blue Anchor, Watchet, Burnham on Sea, Weston super Mare, Clevedon and Portishead. If Somerset folk yearned for a proper blue sea Bournemouth, Weymouth, Lyme Regis, Seaton, Sidmouth and Exmouth could be reached by excursion train. The development of Somerset resorts led to further job opportunities such as a full- or part-time boarding house keeper. Ancillary industries followed – catering and retailing to fulfill the need of the tourist. Seaside shops received many of their goods by rail and the railway's horse-drawn cart or motor lorry made the daily delivery.

Railways played a vital part in the war effort in two World Wars: they carried troops, ammunition and other supplies to the south coast and brought the wounded back to hospital; they brought children to safe areas from cities in the firing line.

How has passenger transport changed between 1847 and 2007? In 1847, as today, not all Somerset settlements were served by rail, and road transport was essential for at least part of the journey. By 1907 many settlements were served by rail, a walk of up to two miles to a station being thought not unreasonable. Railways enabled people to travel across the county, perhaps with the fuss of changing trains at junctions. There was little alternative to rail travel in 1907, but today road travel from one part of the county to another is probably more convenient unless other factors come into the equation: crowded roads, parking problems, lack of driving ability. For longer distances, internal air travel now competes with long distance railway journeys. Because of the closure of local stations except in the Bristol-Bath area, short distance rail commuter traffic is less common than formerly. In 2007 rail travel comes into its own for long distances; it is more restful for the traveller and better for the environment.

Business and holiday travel were present in 1847 and 2007 but special excursion traffic has all but disappeared. Today's trains are of fixed length and inflexible. Until about forty years ago a sudden influx of traffic would produce one or several extra coaches or even a duplicate train. Today, services are run with the minimum number of vehicles to maximise the investment and overcrowding can be a serious complaint.

Rail freight has changed. In 1847 railways were the common carrier and would transport any item from a small parcel to an elephant or tons of coal. In 2007 railways only deal with bulk items – stone from the Mendips and cars and coal from Portbury. A freight train is a relatively rare sight in 2007; the line-side watcher in 1847 or 1907 would have seen as many freight as passenger trains.

And what of the future for the railways of Somerset? Here the author might be permitted to indulge his personal vision. I would like to see more encouragement to use the train, rather than the car, for longer journeys. Free station parking would help, perhaps not in larger towns where people should be encouraged to use the bus to reach the station, but certainly at more rural stations. I would like to see plenty of space on trains, rather than passengers packed in airline style. Space is limited in a car and space could pull people from the car into the train. I don't anticipate many more stations being re-opened because each stop delays a train and if a train is slow people will not use it because it might then be quicker to go by road. And as for commercial use, I would like to see the loads of long-distance lorries carried by rail, road being used only for collection and local distribution. That would bring benefit to the environment.

The scenic potential of the county's branch lines was not sufficiently exploited and it is only now, through the efforts of preservation societies, that localities are realising the economic benefits that a railway can bring to communities. Visitors to preserved railways bring trade to the area when they use shops, hotels, camp-sites and eating places. Although I would like to see more preserved railways I feel that saturation point has been reached, if not over-reached, and that there will be insufficient enthusiasts to run them. Daily steam trains will soon not be a living memory.

And what of those railways closed and not brought back into use? A significant number of them, their formations almost forgotten except perhaps for use as unofficial footpaths, are now becoming official paths and cycle ways offering gentle routes through the heart of the countryside and hopefully away from the sound of road transport.

Suggested Further Reading

Atthill, R, *The Somerset & Dorset Railway* (David & Charles, 1967)

Barrie, D S & Clinker, C R, *The Somerset & Dorset Railway* (Oakwood Press, 1948)

Bradshaw's Railway Guide August 1887, April 1910, July 1922, July 1938 (David & Charles reprints)

Bradshaw's Railway Manual, Sharehholders' Guide and Directory, 1869 (David & Charles reprint)

Clark, R H, *An Historical Survey and Selected Great Western Railway Stations,*

Layouts and Illustrations (Oxford Publishing Co, volume 1 1976, volume 2 1979, volume 3 1981)

Clew, K, *The Somerset Coal Canal and Its Railways* (David & Charles 1970)

Clinker, C R, *Register of Closed Passenger Stations and Goods Depots 1830-1977* (Avon Anglia 1978)

Coleby, I, *The Minehead Branch 1848-1971* (Lightmoor 2006)

Cooke, R A, *Track Layout Diagrams of the Great Western Railway and BR Western Region*, section 15 (1986), 16 (1990), 17 (1983), 18 (1980), 19 (1992), 20 (1988), 21 (1987) (Author)

Hammond, A & C and Derry, R, *Ticket to Minehead* (Millstream 2005)

Harrison, J D, *The Bridgwater Railway* (Oakwood Press 1990)

Hateley, R, *Industrial Railways of South West England* (Industrial Railway Soc. 1977)

Hawkins, M, *The Somerset & Dorset: Then & Now* (David & Charles 1995)

Judge, C W & Potts, C R, *Somerset and Dorset Railways: An Historical Survey of Track Layouts and Illustrations* (Oxford Publishing Co. 1979)

Leitch, R, *The Railways of Keynsham* (RCTS 1997)

MacDermot, E T, revised Clinker, C R, *History of the Great Western Railway* (2 volumes, Ian Allan 1964)

Madge, R, *Railways around Exmoor* (The Exmoor Press 1971/1975)

Somerset Railways (The Dovecote Press 1984)

Maggs, C G, *The Bath to Weymouth Line* (Oakwood Press 1982)

Branch Lines of Somerset (Alan Sutton 1993)

Bristol Railway Panorama (Millstream 1990)

The Clevedon Branch (Wild Swan 1987)

GWR Bristol to Bath Line (Sutton Publishing 2001)

Highbridge in its Heyday (Oakwood Press 1986)

The East Somerset Railway 1858-1998

Celebrating 140 Years (East Somerset Railway 1998)

The Last Years of the Somerset & Dorset (Ian Allan 1991)

The Mangotsfield to Bath Line (Oakwood Press 2005)

The Minehead Branch and the West Somerset Railway (Oakwood Press 1998)

Somerset & Dorset: Life on the Bath to Bournemouth Line (Ian Allen 2007)

Taunton Steam (Millstream 1991)

Weston, Clevedon and Portishead Railway (Oakwood Press 1990)

The Wrington Vale Light Railway (Oakwood Press 2004)

Maggs, C G and Beale, G, *The Camerton Branch* (Wild Swan 1985)

Mitchell, V and Smith, K, (all published by Middleton Press):

Bath Green Park to Bristol (1999)

Bath to Evercreech Junction (1988)

Bournemouth to Evercreech Junction (1987)

Branch Line to Cheddar (1997)

Branch Lines around Chard and Yeovil (1999)

Branch Lines to Clevedon and Portishead (2003)

Branch Line to Minehead (1990)

Bristol to Taunton (2003)

Burnham to Evercreech Junction (1989)

Dorset & Somerset Narrow Gauge (2006)

Frome to Bristol (1986)

Salisbury to Yeovil (1992)

Swindon to Bristol (2002)

Taunton to Barnstaple (1995)

Taunton to Exeter (2002)

Westbury to Bath (1995)

Westbury to Taunton (2002)

Yeovil to Dorchester (1990)

Yeovil to Exeter (1991)

Nock, O S, *History of the Great Western Railway*, volume 3 (Ian Allan 1967)

Oakley, M, *Somerset Railway Stations* (The Dovecote Press 2002)

Peters, I, *The Somerset & Dorset* (Oxford Publishing Co, 1994)

Phillips, D, *Steaming Through the Cheddar Valley* (Ian Allan 2002)

Westbury to Weymouth Line (Oxford Publishing Co, 1994)

Potts, C, *An Historical Survey of Selected Great Western Railway Stations, Layouts and Illustrations* volume 4 (Oxford Publishing Co, 1985)

Pryer, G A, *Track Layout Diagrams of the Southern railway and BR Southern Region Section 5* (R A Cooke 1982)

Robertson, K, *Great Western Railway Halts*, volume 1 (Irwell Press 1990)

volume 2 (KRB Publications 2002)

Sellick, R, *The Old Mineral Line* (The Exmoor Press 1981)

The West Somerset Mineral Railway (David & Charles 1970)

Strange, P, *Weston, Clevedon & Portishead Railway* (Twelveheads Press 1989)

Thomas, D St J, *Regional History of the Railways of Great Britain; volume 1, The West Country* (David & Charles 1981)

Vincent, M, *Reflections on the Portishead Branch* (Oxford Publishing Co, 1983)

Through Countryside and Coalfield (Oxford Publishing Co, 1990)

Williams, R A, *The London & South Western Railway,* volume 2 (David & Charles 1973)